ACCENTURE PLC SHARE CHART (2013 - 2022) IN EUROS

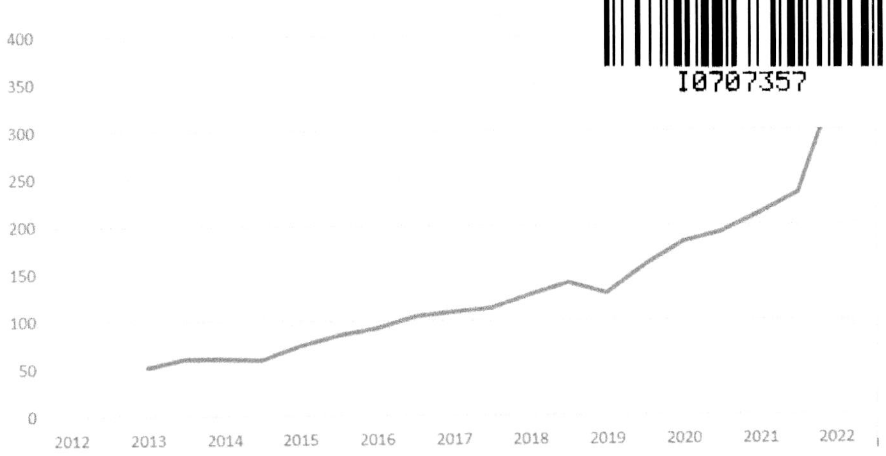

2.   ACUSHNET HOLDINGS CORP

WKN: A2ATTR **ISIN:** US0050981085

333 Bridge Street Fairhaven, MA 02719, **USA**

INTERNET   https://www.acushnetholdingscorp.com

Company

ACUSHNET HOLDINGS CORP is the umbrella company under which the Titleist, FootJoy, Kjus and Pinnacle golf brands are grouped. It is a subsidiary of Fila.

ACUSHNET HOLDINGS has gained **19%** p.a. over the past ten years on average, and 38% over the last 12 months.

The Nasdaq 100 and S&P 500 have gained 8.5% and 7.5% respectively since January 1. **The value of my portfolio has risen by 14% in the same period, i.e. in just over a month and a half, which means that I have outperformed these two indices by 65% and 87% respectively**. The 100 stocks presented in this book **have gained an average of 45% in the last 12 months**. With the stock markets - especially the Nasdaq and the S&P - expected to rise by 30 to 35% this year, you should be able to **expect a 40 to 45% increase in your wealth** if you invest intelligently in the companies that make up the stock selection summarized here.

But that's not all: the shares on this list have an **average annual growth rate of 25% over the last 10 years**. In concrete terms, this means that **in 15 years, 10,000 dollars can become 285,000 dollars or 20,000 dollars can become 570,000 dollars in your account**. And if you already have $100,000 in assets today, they'll probably grow to around **a million in ten years**, and almost **three million in fifteen**.

If you want to become a solid stock market expert, you will find thousands of stock market manuals on the market. However, I am convinced that you don't have to be a financial expert to invest successfully in the stock market. The most important thing is that you compile a list of solid companies that you should monitor regularly so that you are prepared to invest in the right one(s) at the right time.

Finally, a note: you can find 120 other excellent company shares in my other books, which can also be purchased from **Amazon©**.

1. ACCENTURE PLC

WKN: A0YAQA **ISIN:** IE00B4BNMY34

Grand Canal Square, Grand Canal Harbour 1 Dublin 2,
Ireland

Internet http://www.accenture.com

Company

ACCENTURE PLC is a global consulting firm. The group provides management consulting, technology and outsourcing services to businesses and governments worldwide. Its expertise spans all industries and management areas. The consulting portfolio is divided into the industry segments "Communications, Media & Technology", "Financial Services", "Health & Public Service", "Products" and "Resources".

ACCENTURE has gained **23% p.a.** over the past ten years on average, and 34% over the last 12 months.

ACUSHNET HOLDINGS share chart (2018- 2023) in US-Dollar

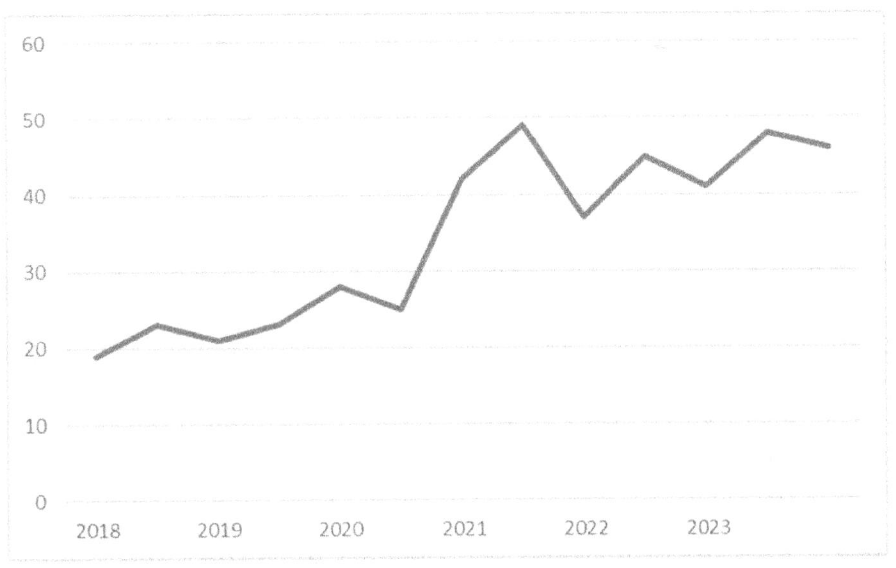

3. ADVANCED DRAINAGE SYSTEMS INC.

WKN: -- ISIN: US00790R1041

4640 Trueman Blvd, Hilliard, OH 43026, **USA**

INTERNET   HTTP://WWW.ADSPIPE.COM

Company

ADVANCED DRAINAGE SYSTEMS INC. designs, manufactures and markets polypropylene and polyethylene pipe, plastic leach field chambers and systems, septic tanks and accessories, storm detention/retention and septic chambers, polyvinyl chloride drainage structures, fittings, and water filters and separators.

Over the past ten years, ADVANCED DRAINAGE SYSTEMS has gained an average of **25% p.a.**, and 84% over the last 12 months.

ADVANCED DRAINAGE SYSTEMS INC. share chart (2012 - 2022) in US-dollar

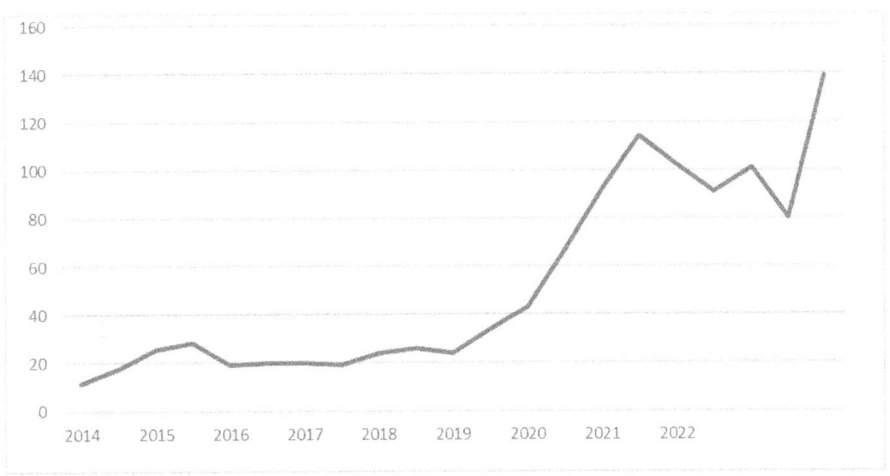

4. ADVANCED MICRO DEVICES INC.

WKN: 863186 ISIN: US0079031078

Augustine Drive 2485 95054 Santa Clara, CA, **USA**

Internet http://www.amd.com

Company

ADVANCED MICRO DEVICES INC. (AMD) helps leading computer, wireless and consumer electronics companies deliver high-performance, energy-efficient solutions to their customers. The company produces processors, graphics cards and complete chipsets for computers, game consoles and telecommunications devices. The chip producer holds more than 4500 patents.

In the past ten years ADVANCED MICRO DEVICES has gained **42% p.a.** on average, and 108% over the last 12 months.

ADVANCED MICRO DEVICES INC. share chart (2012 - 2022) in euros

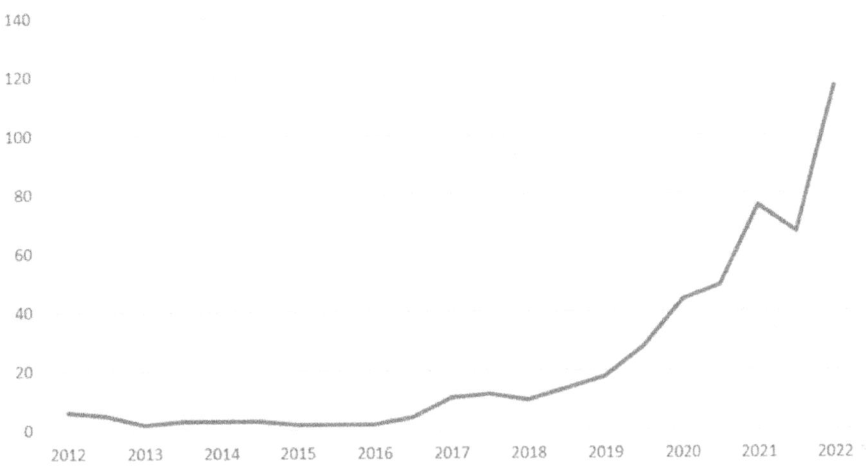

5.   AIR LIQUIDE SA

WKN: 850133 **ISIN:** FR0000120073

Quai d'Orsay 75 75321 Paris, **FRANCE**

INTERNET   https://www.airliquide.com

Company

AIR LIQUIDE SA is an internationally present manufacturer of industrial gases and liquid gases for medical applications. The gases, such as oxygen, nitrogen, argon and hydrogen, are used in oil and steel processing, in paper and glass production, as well as in healthcare or the semiconductor and photovoltaic industries. The Group is divided into three divisions: Gas & Services, Engineering & Construction and Global Markets & Technologies. AIR LIQUIDE SA has expanded its business activities to more than 80 countries.

Over the past ten years AIR LIQUIDE has gained **9% p.a.** on average, and 29% over the last 12 months.

AIR LIQUIDE share chart (2013 - 2023) in euros

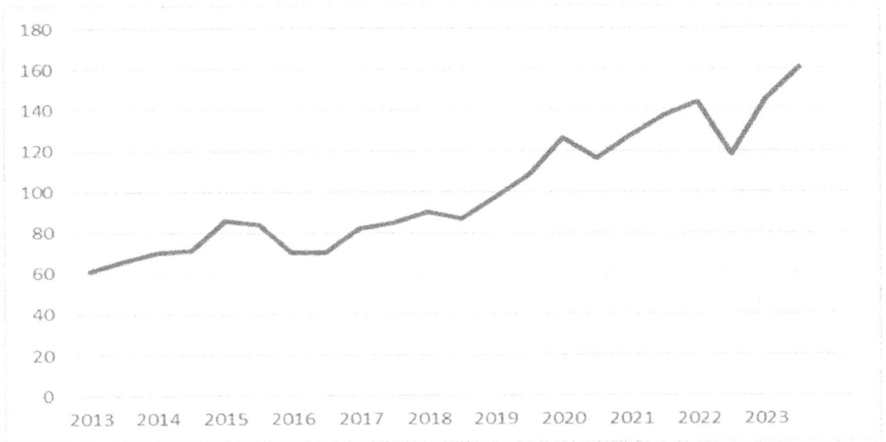

6.   AIRBUS GROUP

WKN: 938914 **ISIN:** NL0000235190

B80 Building, 2, rond-point Dewoitine, BP 90112 31703 Blagnac, **FRANCE**

INTERNET   https://www.airbus.com

Company

AIRBUS GROUP is one of the world's two largest manufacturers of commercial aircraft, civil helicopters, commercial space launch vehicles and missiles, and the largest aerospace company in Europe. The company also holds a leading position in military aircraft, satellites and defense electronics. AIRBUS GROUP includes the civil aircraft manufacturer Airbus, the helicopter manufacturer Eurocopter and the space company Astrium.The Group operates in more than 170 locations worldwide and is increasingly expanding its activities outside Europe.

Over the past ten years, AIRBUS has gained **10% p.a.** on average, and 22% over the last 12 months.

.

AIRBUS GROUP share chart (2013 - 2023) in euros

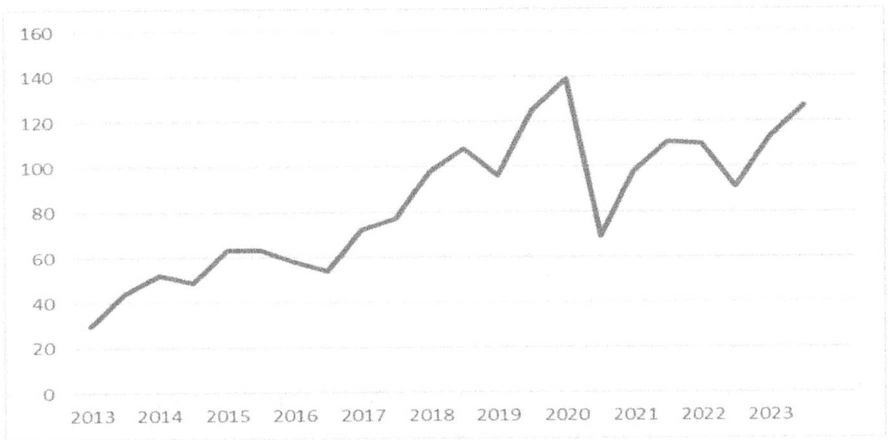

7. ALPHABET INC.

WKN: A14Y6H ISIN: US02079K1079

Amphitheatre Parkway 1600 94043 Mountain View, CA, **USA**

Internet http://www.abc.xyz

Company

ALPHABET INC. (previously Google Inc.) is an Internet service provider that started out as a pure search engine. Today, ALPHABET INC. stands for a range of other services ALPHABET 's well-known applications include Google, Google Maps, Google Earth, YouTube or Android. In October 2015, ALPHABET INC. to allow the individual parts of the company, such as the web business (still under the Google name) or the development of self-driving cars, to operate more independently as individual subsidiaries.

Over the past decade, ALPHABET (Google) gained **26% p.a.** on average, and 51% over the last 12 months.

ALPHABET INC. (previously GOOGLE INC.) share chart (2012 - 2022) in euros

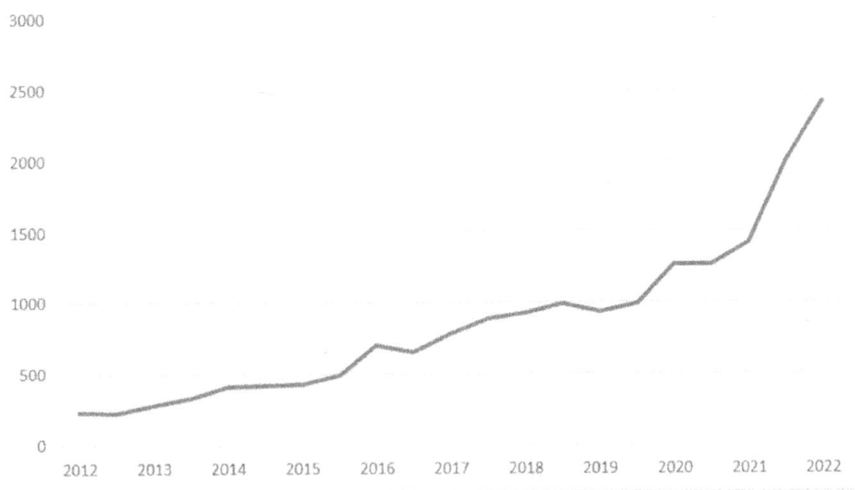

8.   ALTAIR ENGINEERING INC.

WKN: A2DYPC **ISIN:** US0213691035

1820 E. Big Beaver Rd. Troy, MI 48083, **USA**

INTERNET   https://altair.com

Company

ALTAIR ENGINEERING INC. provides open architecture solutions for data analytics and artificial intelligence (AI), computer-aided engineering, and high-performance computing (HPC) that enable the development and optimization of high-performance, innovative, and sustainable products and processes.

Over the past six years, ALTAIR ENGINEERING has gained **27% p.a.** on average, and 31% over the last 12 months.

ALTAIR ENGINEERING INC. share chart (2017 - 2023) in euros

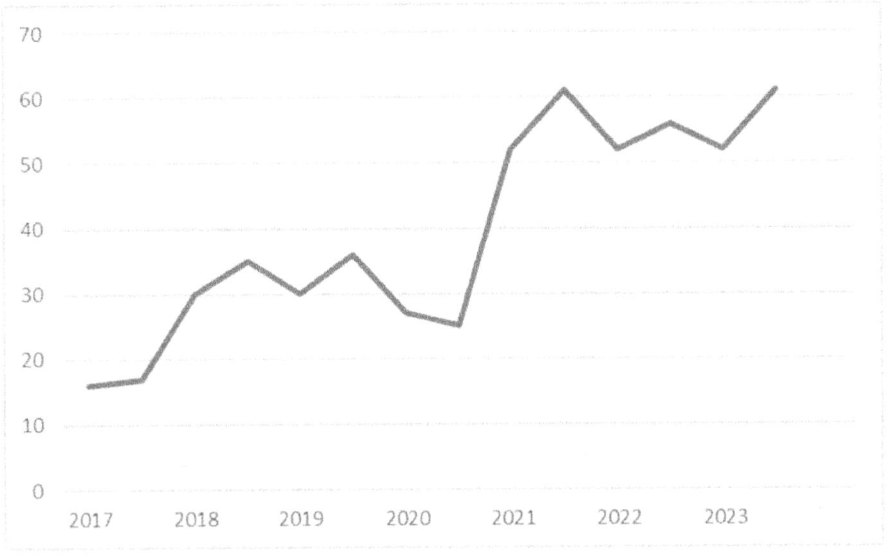

9.   AMAZON.COM INC.

WKN: 906866 ISIN: US0231351067

Terry Avenue North 410 98109-5210 Seattle, WA, **USA**

Internet http://www.amazon.com

Company

AMAZON.COM INC. is the world's largest online retailer. AMAZON.COM INC. targets its products and services to end customers as well as sellers, businesses and content creators.

Over the past ten years, AMAZON.COM has gained **33% p.a.** on average, and 74% over the last 12 months.

AMAZON.COM INC. share chart (2012 - 2022) in euros

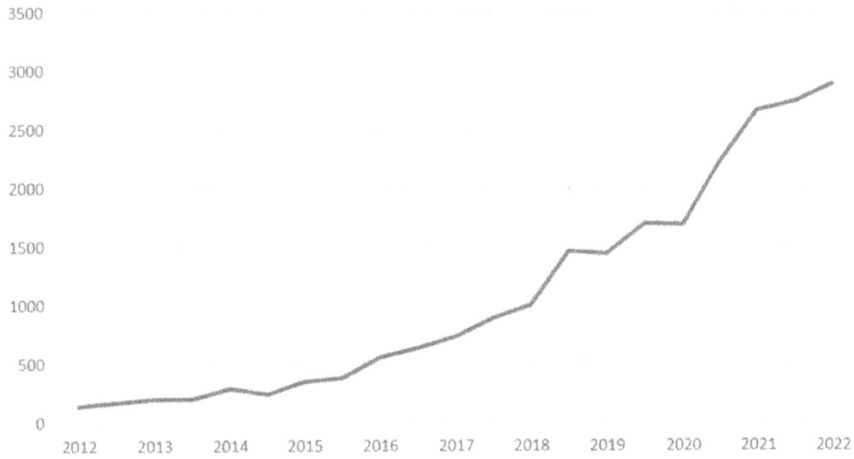

10. AMERIPRISE FINANCIAL INC.

WKN: A0F55S **ISIN:** US03076C1062

753 Ameriprise Financial Ctr, Minneapolis, MN 55474, **USA**

INTERNET   https://ir.ameriprise.com

Company

AMERIPRISE FINANCIAL INC. provides financial planning, liquidity, wealth accumulation, income, protection, and estate and wealth transfer products and services. Within the U.S., Ameriprise markets its products and solutions through three primary brands: Ameriprise Financial, Columbia Management and RiverSource. In the international market, wealth management solutions are marketed through the Threadneedle brand.

Over the past ten years AMERIPRISE FINANCIAL has gained **15% p.a.** on average, and 17% over the last 12 months.

AMERIPRISE FINANCIAL INC. share chart (2016 - 2023) in euros

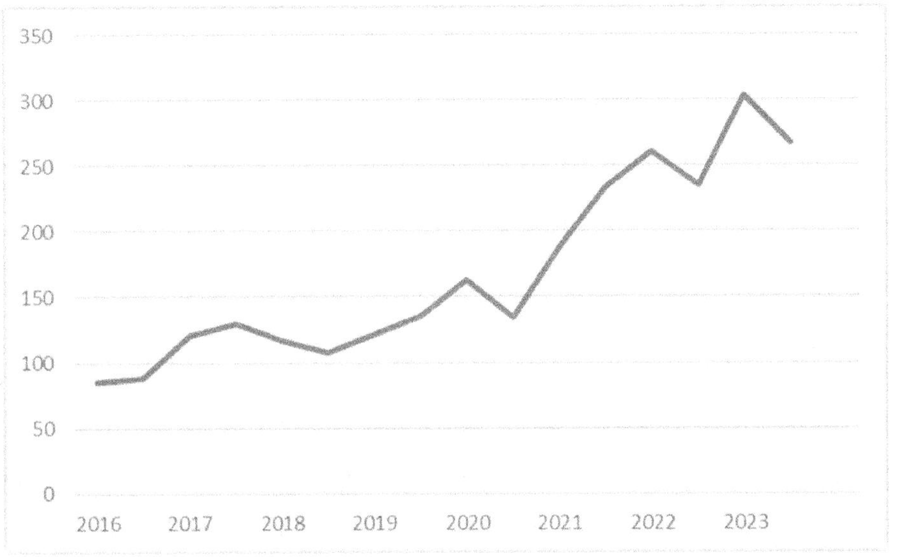

11.   AMETEK INC.

WKN: 908668 ISIN: US0311001004

Cassatt Road 1100 19312-1177 Berwyn, PA, **USA**

Internet http://www.ametek.com

Company

AMETEK INC. is an American global leader in the manufacture of electric motors and electronic instruments. AMETEK INC.'s products are used, for example, in blowers, pumps, nuclear instrumentation, microanalysis systems for scanning and transmission electron microscopes, micro-XRF benchtop instruments for non-destructive elemental analysis, high-speed cameras, and fixed infrared thermometer systems. The group has operations in North America, Europe, Asia and South America.

In the past ten years, AMETEK has gained **18% p.a.** on average, and 20% over the last 12 months.

AMETEK INC.share chart (2012 - 2022) in euros

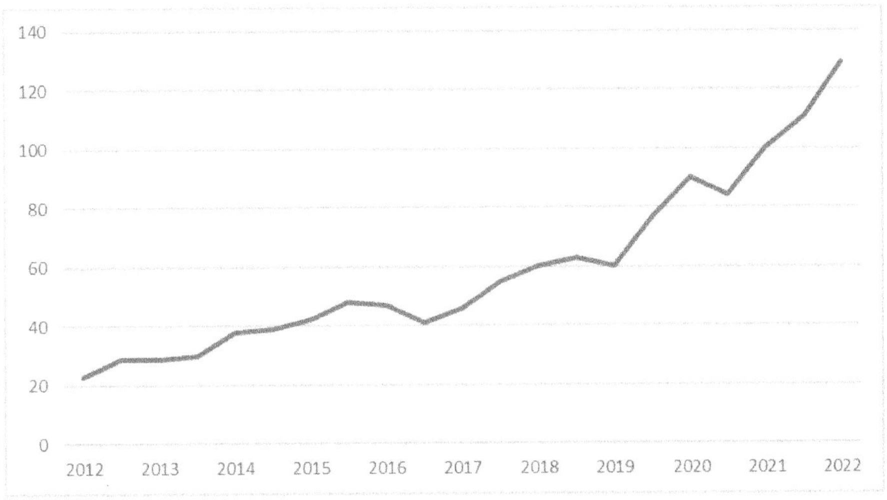

12. AMPHENOL CORP.

WKN: 882749 ISIN: US0320951017

Hall Avenue 358 06492 Wallingford, CT, **USA**

Internet http://www.amphenol.com

Company

AMPHENOL CORP. is one of the world's largest manufacturers of connectors. The company designs, manufactures and markets electrical, electronic and fiber optic connectors, interconnect systems, antennas, sensors and sensor-based products, and coaxial and high-speed specialty cables. It has a diversified presence in high-growth markets such as automotive, broadband communications, commercial aerospace, industrial, information technology and data communications, military, mobile devices and cellular networks.

Over the past ten years, AMPHENOL has gained **19% p.a.** on average, and 28% over the last 12 months.

AMPHENOL CORP. share chart (2012 - 2022) in euros

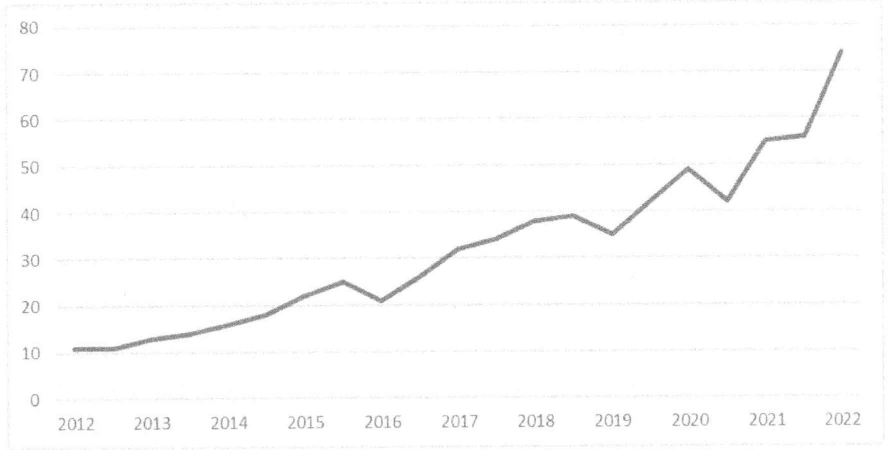

13.   AMPLIFON SPA

WKN: A0JMJX ISIN: IT0004056880

Via G. Ripamonti 133 20141 Milan, **Italy**

Internet http://corporate.amplifon.com/

Company

AMPLIFON SPA specializes in the sale and fitting of hearing solutions and the fitting of personalized products. The company operates in 29 countries around the world with approximately 11,000 points of sale. The business is divided into three specific geographic areas, which comprise the Group's operating segments: Europe, Middle East and Africa, Americas and Asia-Pacific.

Over the past ten years, AMPLIFON has gained an average of **30% p.a.**, and 16% over the last 12 months.

AMPLIFON SPA share chart (2012 - 2022) in euros

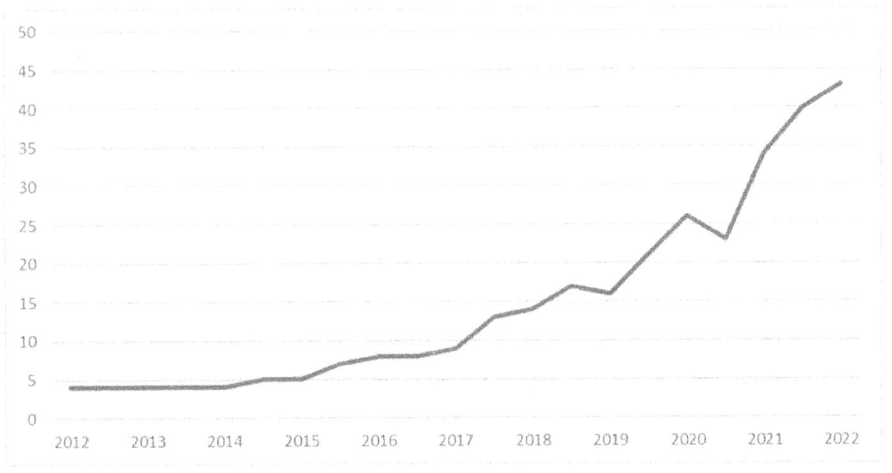

14.   APPLE INC.

WKN: 865985 **ISIN:** US0378331005

One Apple Park Way Cupertino, California 95014, **USA**

INTERNET   https://www.apple.com/

Company

APPLE INC. designs, manufactures and sells smartphones, PCs, tablets, wearables and accessories, as well as a variety of cloud services. APPLE INC. also sells related software, peripherals, networking products, and digital content and apps.

In the past ten years APPLE has gained **28% p.a.** on average, and 23% over the last 12 months.

APPLE INC. share chart (2013 - 2023) in euros

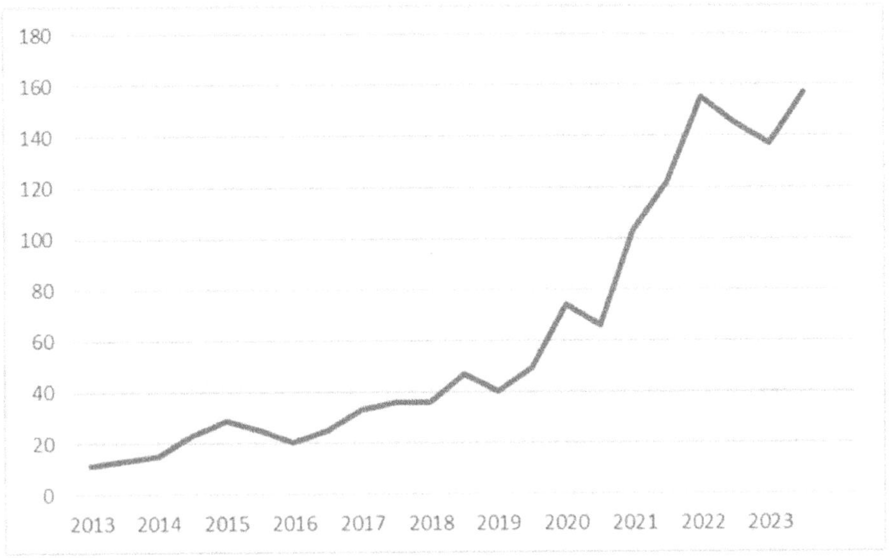

15.   APPLIED MATERIALS INC.

WKN: 865177 **ISIN:** US0382221051

Bowers Avenue 3050 95052-8039 Santa Clara, CA, **USA**

INTERNET   https://ir.appliedmaterials.com/

Company

APPLIED MATERIALS INC. is a leading global supplier to the semiconductor, flat panel display and solar industries. The company's solutions are used in the manufacture of products such as smartphones, flat-panel TVs and solar panels. APPLIED MATERIALS INC.'s range of products and services also includes turnkey factories for the production of solar cells.

In the past ten years, APPLIED MATERIALS has gained **24% p.a.** on average, and 74% over the last 12 months.

APPLIED MATERIALS INC. share chart (2013 – 2023) in euros

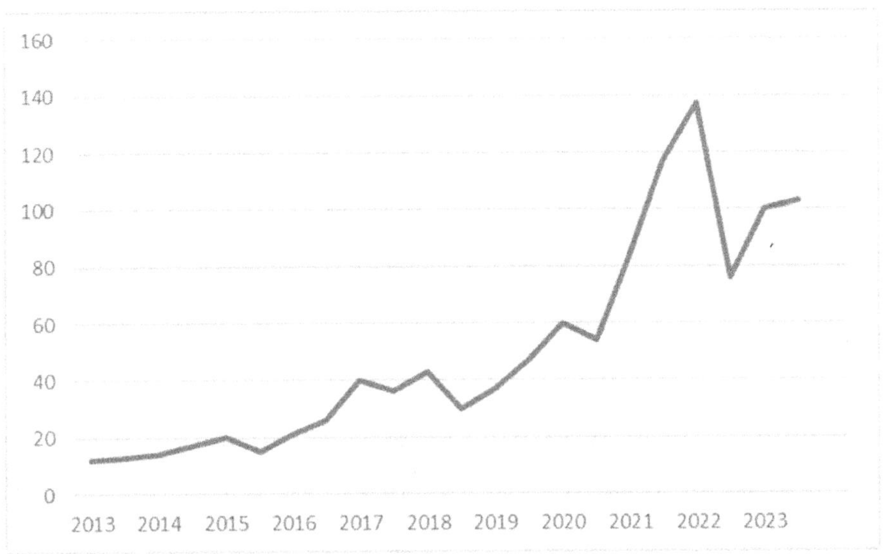

16.   ASML HOLDING NV

WKN: A1J4U4 **ISIN:** NL0010273215

De Run 6501 5504 DR Veldhoven, **THE NETHERLANDS**

INTERNET   https://www.asml.com

Company

ASML HOLDING NV is in the production of optical lithography systems for the semiconductor industry. The company manufactures complex machines for the production of chips and integrated circuits (IC). The Group is active in the design, development, production and marketing and provides complementary services. Worldwide, ASML HOLDING NV is active in over 60 locations in 16 countries.

In the past ten years, ASML HOLDING has gained **25% p.a.** on average, and 49% over the last 12 months.

ASML HOLDING NV share chart (2013 - 2023) in euros

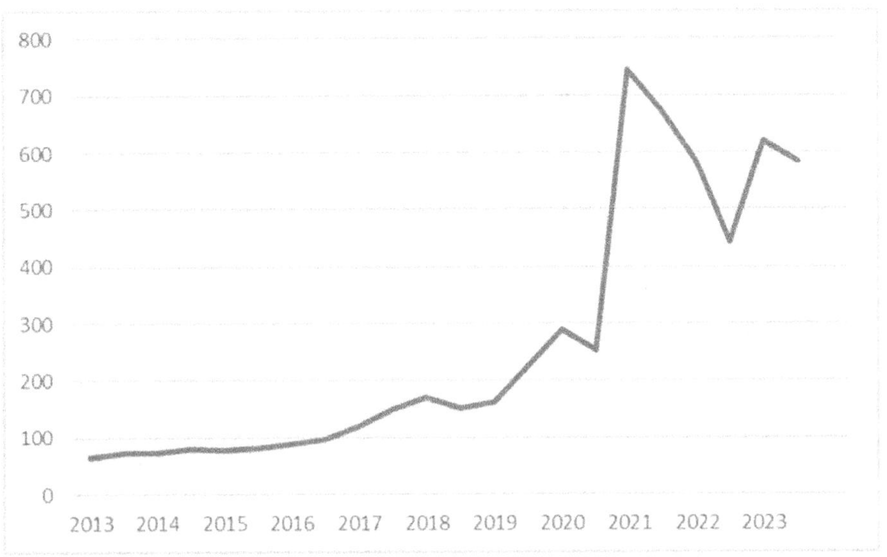

17.   ATOSS SOFTWARE AG

WKN: 510440 ISIN: DE0005104400

Am Moosfeld 3 81829 Munich, **Germany**

Internet http://www.atoss.com

Company

ATOSS SOFTWARE AG is one of the leading providers of software solutions in the field of strategic personnel deployment in Germany. The solution portfolio comprises the areas of working time management, staff efficiency management, personnel resource planning, business process management, special solutions for medium-sized companies as well as customer-oriented consulting.

Over the past ten years, ATOSS SOFTWARE has gained an average of **36 % p.a**, and 45% over the last 12 months.

ATOSS SOFTWARE AG share chart (2012 - 2022) in euros

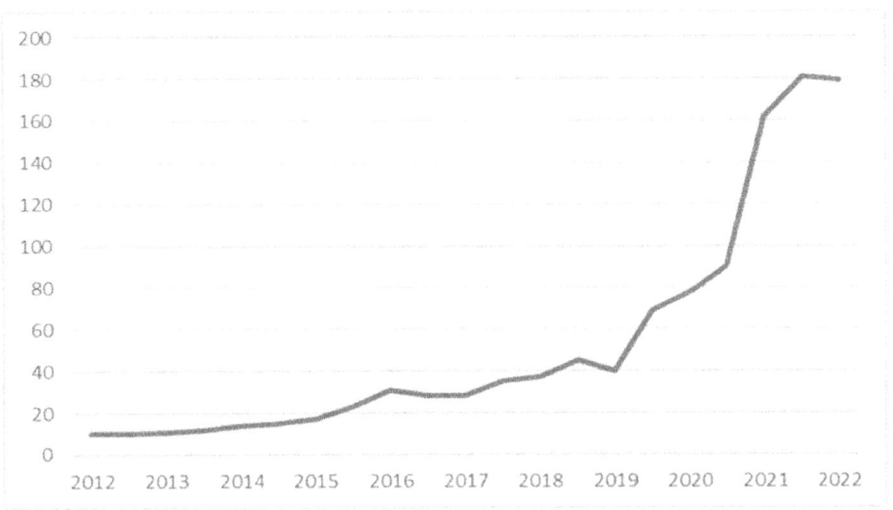

18.   AUTODESK INC.

WKN: 869964 **ISIN:** US0527691069

McInnis Parkway 111 94903 San Rafael, CA, **USA**

INTERNET   https://www.autodesk.com/

Company

AUTODESK INC. develops and distributes software in the areas of 3D design, engineering and entertainment software. AUTODESK INC. develops and distributes software in the areas of 3D design, engineering and entertainment software. Content is also offered by AUTODESK INC. The company is active in the fields of engineering, architecture, construction, geographic information systems and multimedia, as well as product design and development. AutoCAD is the company's flagship product.

Over the past ten years, AUTODESK has gained **19% p.a.** on average, and 30% over the last 12 months.

AUTODESK INC. share chart (2013 - 2023) in euros

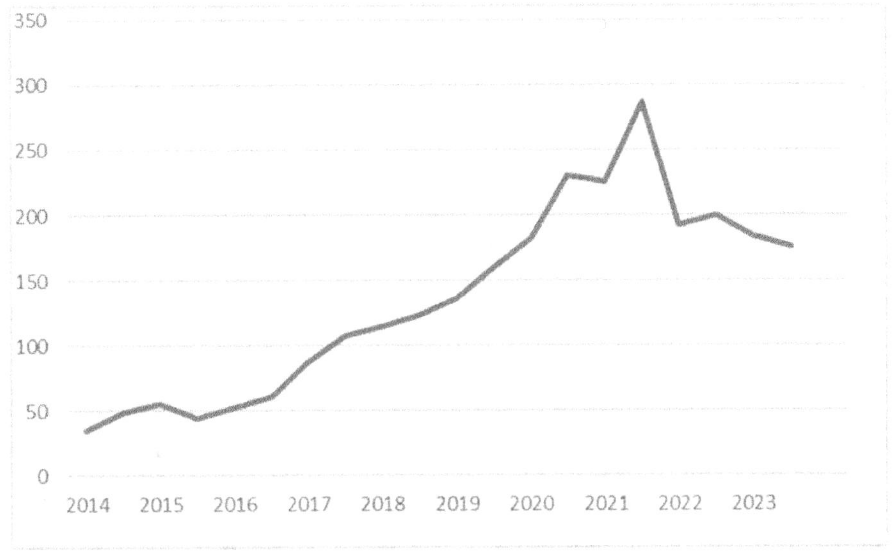

19.   BADGER METER INC.

WKN: 863871 **ISIN:** US0565251081

4545 West Brown Deer Road; 53223-2413 Milwaukee, **USA**

INTERNET   http://www.badgermeter.com

Company

BADGER METER INC. is a leading designer and manufacturer of flow measurement, quality, control and communication solutions. The company provides mechanical or static water meters and related radio and software technologies and services, and water flow meters for hydroelectric power plants and wastewater treatment plants. The company sells its products primarily in the US.

In the past ten years, BADGER METER has gained an average of **21% p.a.**, and 31% over the last 12 months.

BADGER METER INC. share chart (2013 - 2023) in euros

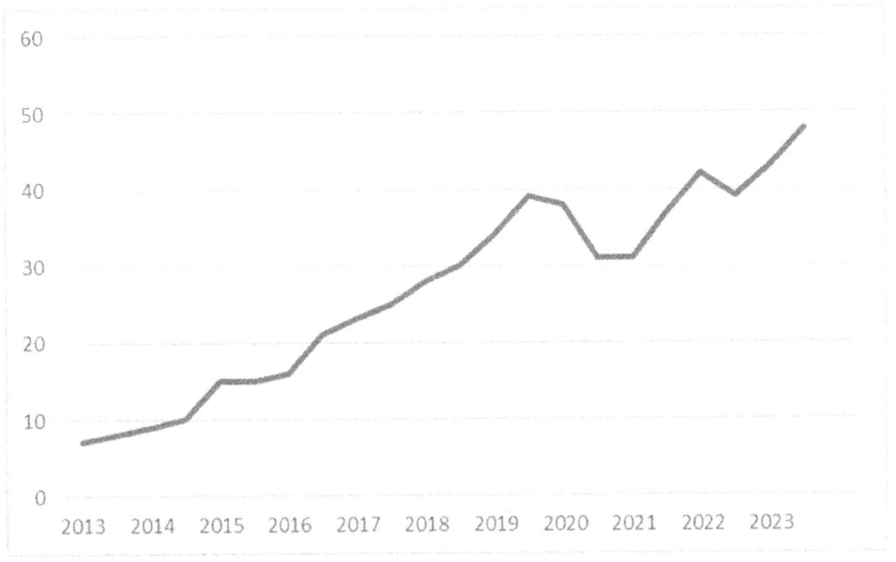

20.   BECHTLE AG

WKN: 515870 **ISIN:** DE0005158703

Bechtle Platz 1 74172 Neckarsulm, **GERMANY**

INTERNET   https://www.bechtle.com

Company

With around 80 system house locations in Germany, Austria and Switzerland and 24 e-commerce companies in 14 countries, BECHTLE AG is Europe's largest IT system house and the leading IT e-commerce provider in Europe. The company is networked worldwide through IT alliance partners on all continents.

Over the past ten years, BECHTLE has gained an average of **19% p.a.**, and 23% over the last 12 months.

BECHTLE AG share chart (2013 - 2023) in euros

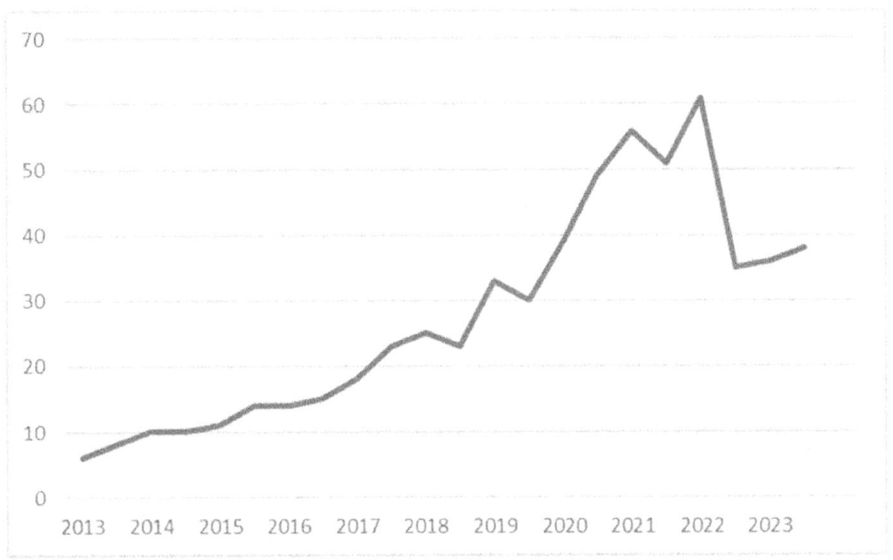

21.   BERKSHIRE HATHAWAY INC.

WKN: A0YJQ2 ISIN: US08467026

3555 Farnam Street, Suite 1440 68131 Omaha, NE, **USA**

Internet http://www.berkshirehathaway.com

Company

BERKSHIRE HATHAWAY INC. is the investment holding company of Warren E. Buffett. It invests only in promising companies with low debt and a clear business model. The investment portfolio covers a wide range of insurance services (property, casualty, health and life insurance). The insurance and reinsurance businesses form the backbone of BERKSHIRE HATHAWAY INC., but the holding also includes companies in other industries, such as Fruit of the Loom (apparel), R.C. Wiley (furniture) and See's Candies (confectionery). In addition, BERKSHIRE HATHAWAY INC. holds investments in companies such as Coca-Cola, Gillette, the Washington Post and Munich Re.

Over the past ten years, BERKSHIRE HATHAWAY has gained an average of **15% p.a.**, and 34% over the last 12 months.

BERKSHIRE HATHAWAY INC. share chart (2012 - 2022) in euros

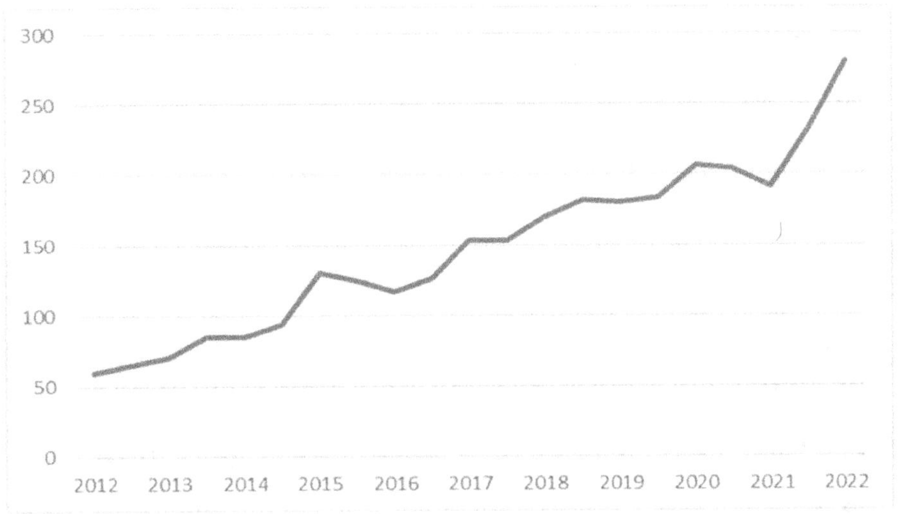

22.   BOSTON SCIENTIFIC CORP.

WKN: 884113 **ISIN:** US1011371077

Boston Scientific Way 300 01752-1234, Marlborough, MA,
USA

INTERNET   https://www.bostonscientific.com

Company

BOSTON SCIENTIFIC CORP. develops, manufactures and markets products used in a range of specialty medical treatments including cardiology, electrophysiology, gastroenterology, neurovascular intervention, pulmonary medicine, radiology, oncology, urology and vascular medicine.

Over the past ten years, BOSTON SCIENTIFIC has gained an average of **19% p.a**, and 40% over the last 12 months.

BOSTON SCIENTIFIC CORP. share chart (2013 - 2023) in euros

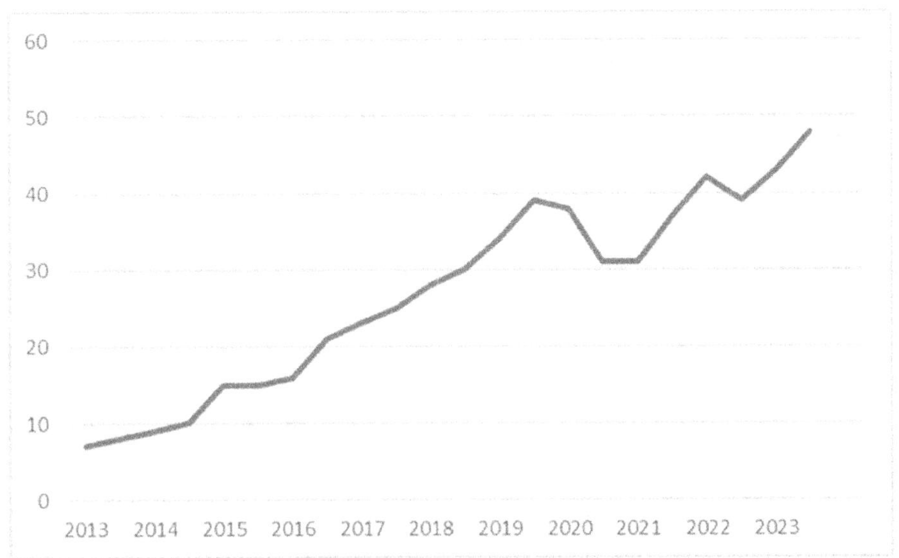

23.   BROADCOM INC.

WKN: 11135F101 ISIN: US11135F1012

1320 Ridder Park Drive San Jose, California 95131, **USA**

Internet http://www.broadcom.com

Company

BROADCOM INC. is a leading manufacturer of integrated circuits or network adapters and devices for data transmission. The company produces highly integrated chips that enable broadband communications and the transmission of audio, video and data. BROADCOM INC. offers complete system-on-a-chip solutions. The product range includes solutions for digital cable, satellite or Internet protocols, set-top boxes, HDTV devices, smartphones, GPS as well as cable or DSL modems and chips for mobile communications.

Over the past ten years, BROADCOM has gained an average of **37% p.a.,** and 105% over the last 12 months.

BROADCOM INC. share chart (2012 - 2022) in US dollars

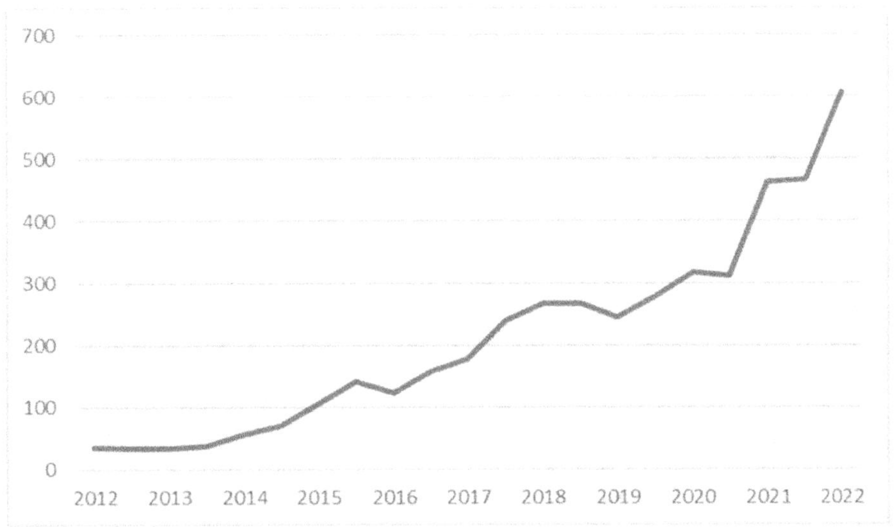

24.   BROADRIDGE FINANCIAL SOLUTIONS INC.

WKN: A0MMP1 ISIN: US11133T1034

Dakota Drive 5, Suite 300 11042 Lake Success, New York,
USA

Internet http://www.broadridge.com

Company

BROADRIDGE FINANCIAL SOLUTIONS INC. is a leading global financial technology company that provides investor communications and technology-enabled solutions to banks, broker-dealers, asset managers and corporate issuers. Its primary business is as a service provider to public companies producing annual reports and other financial documents.

Over the past decade, BROADRIDGE FINANCIAL SOLUTIONS has gained an average of **25% p.a.**, and 37% over the last 12 months.

BROADRIDGE FINANCIAL SOLUTIONS INC. share chart (2012 - 2022) in euros

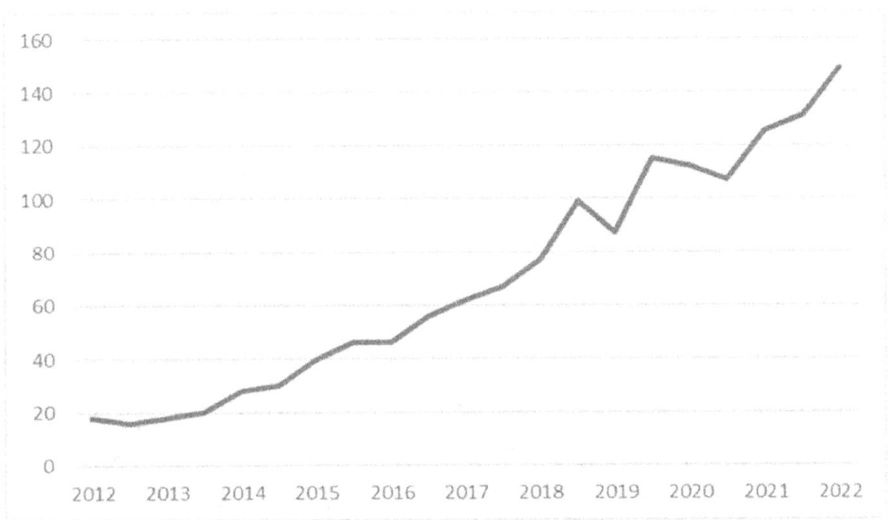

25.   CADENCE DESIGN SYSTEMS INC.

WKN: 873567 ISIN: US1273871087

Seely Avenue 2655 95134 San Jose, California, **USA**

Internet   http://www.cadence.com

Company

CADENCE DESIGN SYSTEMS INC. provides products, consulting services and design services for the automation and efficient management of design processes for semiconductors, computer systems, networking and telecommunications systems, consumer electronics and a variety of other electronic products.

Over the past ten years, CADENCE DESIGN SYSTEMS has gained an average of **31% p.a.,** and 47% over the last 12 months.

CADENCE DESIGN SYSTEMS INC.share chart (2017 - 2022) in euros

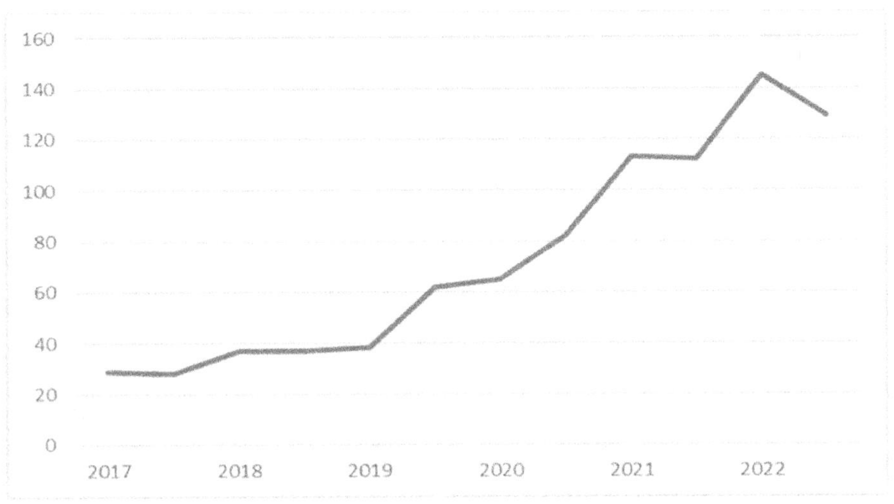

26. CAPGEMINI SE

WKN: 869858 ISIN: FR0000125338

Rue de Tilsitt 11 75017 Paris, **France**

Internet   http://www.capgemini.com

Company

CAPGEMINI SE is a global leader in management and IT consulting, technology and outsourcing. With a focus on consulting for the development and implementation of growth strategies and the use of new technologies, the business activities are divided into the Consulting Services, Outsourcing Services, Technology Services and Local Professional Services (Sogeti) divisions. The Consulting Services division supports companies with strategy and management consulting to optimize their business processes and increase performance.

Over the past ten years, CAPGEMINI has gained an average of **19% p.a.**, and 20% over the last 12 months.

CAPGEMINI SE share chart (2012 - 2022) in euros

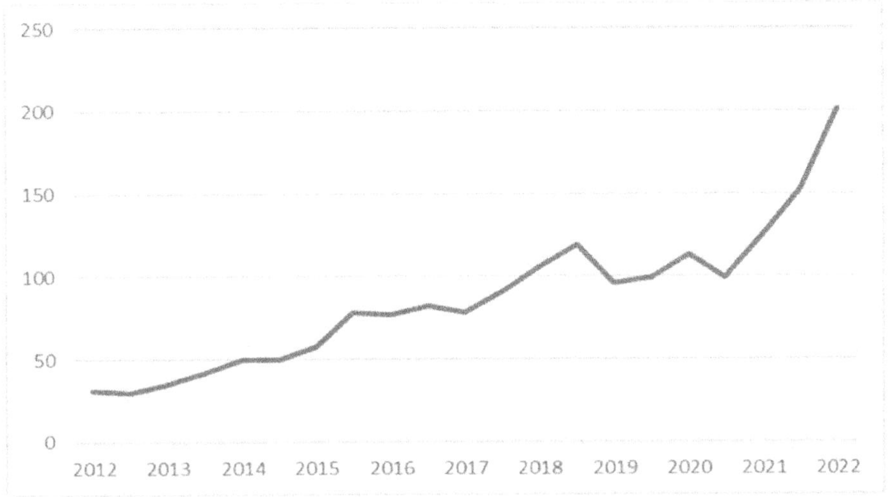

27.   CASELLA WASTE SYSTEMS INC.

WKN: 910249 ISIN: US1474481041

25 Greens Hill Lane, Rutland, Vermont, **USA**

Internet   https://www.casella.com

Company

CASELLA WASTE SYSTEMS INC. is a regional, vertically integrated solid waste services company. CASELLA WASTE SYSTEMS INC. provides resource management expertise and services to residential, commercial, municipal and industrial customers, primarily in the areas of solid waste collection and disposal, transfer, recycling and organics services.

Over the past ten years, CASELLA WASTE SYSTEMS has gained an average of **19% p.a.**, and 17% over the last 12 months.

CASELLA WASTE SYSTEMS INC. share chart (2018 - 2022) in euros

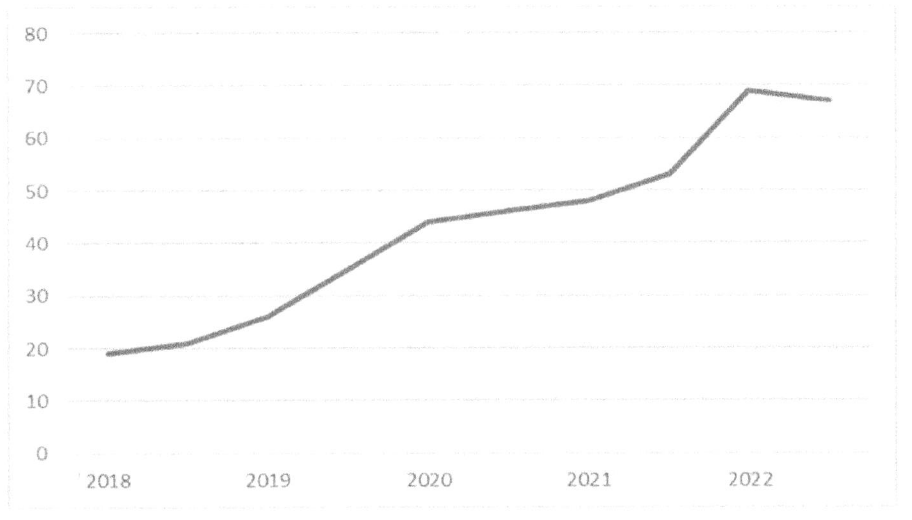

28. CDW CORP.

WKN: 12514G108 ISIN: US12514G1085

75 Tri-State International Lincolnshire, IL 60069, **USA**

Internet   https://www.cdw.com/

Company

CDW CORP. is a leading provider of hardware and software products to IT solutions for mobility, security, data center optimization, cloud computing and virtualization for business, government, education and healthcare.

Over the past nine years, CDW has gained an average of **32% p.a.**, and 16% over the last 12 months.

CDW CORP. share chart (2013 - 2022) in US dollars

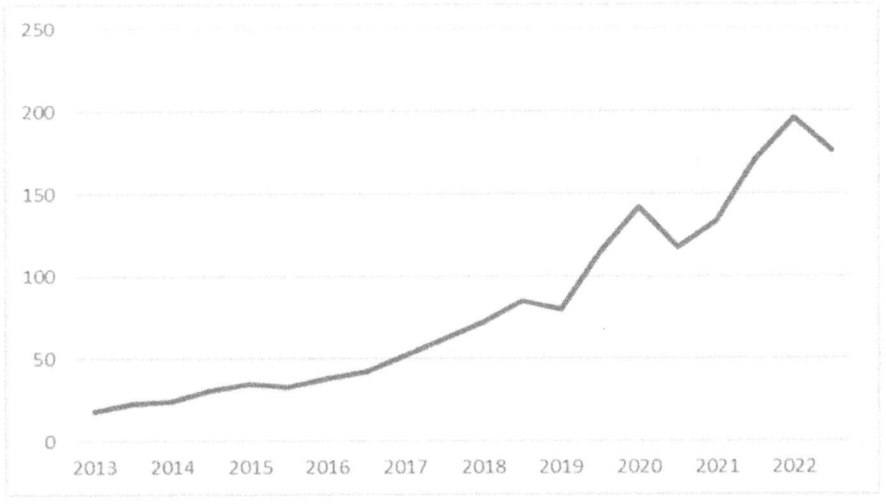

29. CINTAS CORP.

WKN: 880205 ISIN: US1729081059

Cintas Boulevard 6800 45262-5737 Cincinnati, OH, **USA**

Internet   http://www.cintas.com

Company

CINTAS CORP. is a U.S. textile company that designs and manufactures professional uniforms for all types of companies in all industries, tailored to corporate identity upon request, and rents or sells them to companies of various sizes and in a variety of industries. The company's products are distributed in North America and Latin America, as well as in Asia and Europe. The company operates more than 390 facilities in the U.S. and Canada including four manufacturing and eight distribution centers. Furthermore, the company's product line also includes first aid kits, safety and fire protection products, and document services.

Over the past ten years, CINTAS has gained an average of **28% p.a.**, and 41% over the last 12 months.

CINTAS CORP. share chart (2012 - 2022) in euros

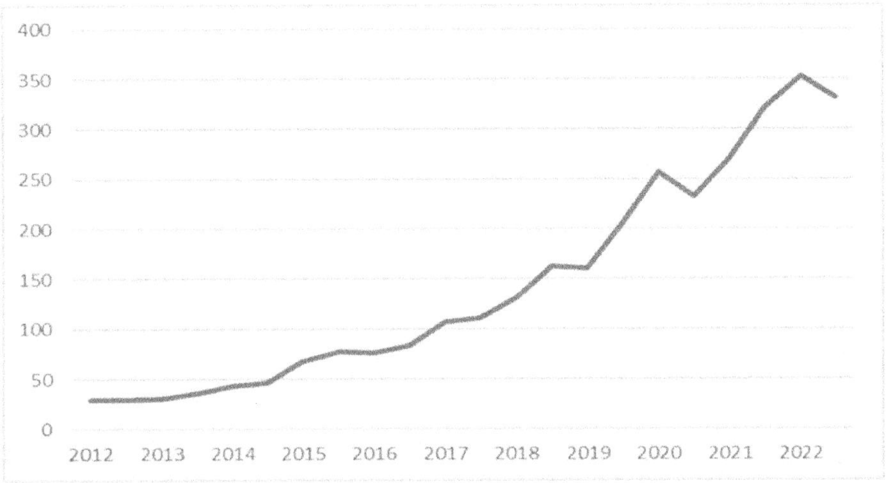

30.   COMFORT SYSTEMS USA INC.

WKN: 907784 ISIN: US1999081045

675 Bering Dr. Suite 400 Houston, TX 77057, **USA**

Internet   https://comfortsystemsusa.com

Company

COMFORT SYSTEMS USA INC. is a leading building and service provider for mechanical, electrical and plumbing building systems. COMFORT SYSTEMS USA INC. disposes of an expertise in mechanical and electrical services, process piping, modular construction, controls, energy efficiency and countless other nonresidential building renovation and service needs.

Over the past ten years, COMFORT SYSTEMS USA has gained an average of **24% p.a.**, and 94% over the last 12 months.

COMFORT SYSTEMS USA INC. share chart (2012 - 2022) in euros

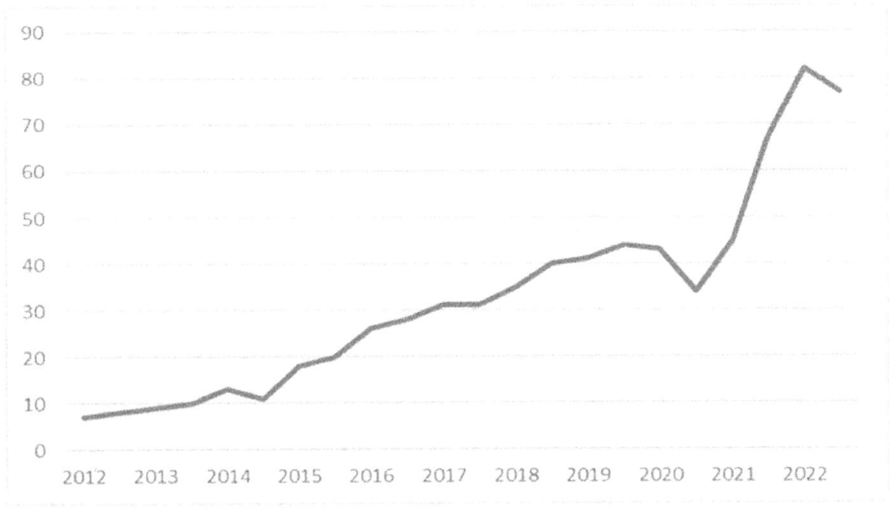

31. CONSTELLATION SOFTWARE INC.

WKN: A0JM27 ISIN: CA21037X1006

Adelaide Street East 20, Suite 1200 M5C 2T6 Tornto, Ontario, **CANADA**

Internet   http://www.csisoftware.com

Company

CONSTELLATION SOFTWARE INC. provides market-leading software and services to diverse industries in the public and private sectors. The company develops industry-specific software that is tailored to customers' unique needs with specific mission-critical solutions. CONSTELLATION SOFTWARE INC. serves more than 85,000 customers in over 100 countries.

Over the past ten years, CONSTELLATION SOFTWARE has gained an average of **34% p.a.**, and 55% over the last 12 months.

Over the past ten years, SYNOPSYS has gained an average of **32% p.a.**

CONSTELLATION SOFTWARE INC. share chart (2016 - 2022) in euros

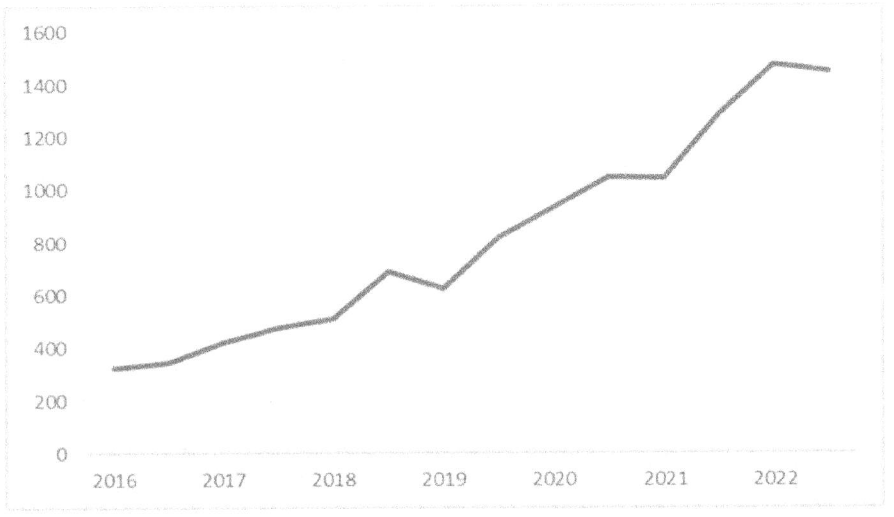

32.   CORVEL CORP.

WKN: 221006109 ISIN: US2210061097

2010 Main Street Suite 600 Irvine, CA 92614, **USA**

Internet   https://www.corvel.com

Company

CORVEL CORP. is a provider of risk management solutions for the workers' compensation, auto, health and disability management industries. CORVEL CORP. provides clients with the information and insight they need to make decisions in these fields.

Over the past ten years, CORVEL has gained an average of **24% p.a.**, and 39% over the last 12 months.

CORVEL CORP. share chart (2012 - 2022) in US dollars

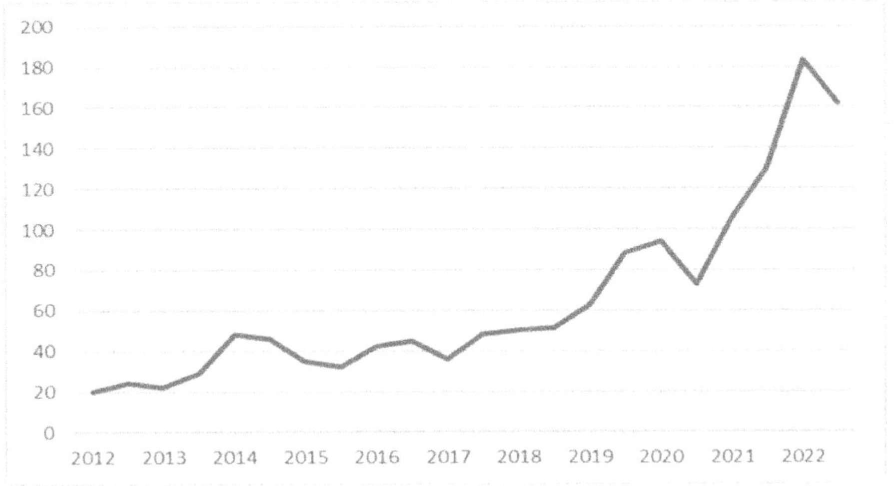

33.   COSTCO WHOLESALE CORP.

WKN: 22160K105 ISIN: US22160K1051

Lake Drive 999 98027 Issaquah, WA, **USA**

Internet   http://www.costco.com

Company

COSTCO WHOLESALE CORP. operates more than 600 independently owned and operated self-service department stores in the U.S., U.K., Japan, Mexico, Taiwan, Korea, Australia and Canada, and supplies small stores or businesses with special offers on limited and select branded products. Merchandise ranges from food and cosmetics, computers, electrical and household appliances to furniture, clothing, jewelry and pet food.

Over the past ten years, COSTCO WHOLESALE has gained an average of **20% p.a.**, and 43% over the last 12 months.

COSTCO WHOLESALE CORP. share chart (2012 - 2022) in US dollars

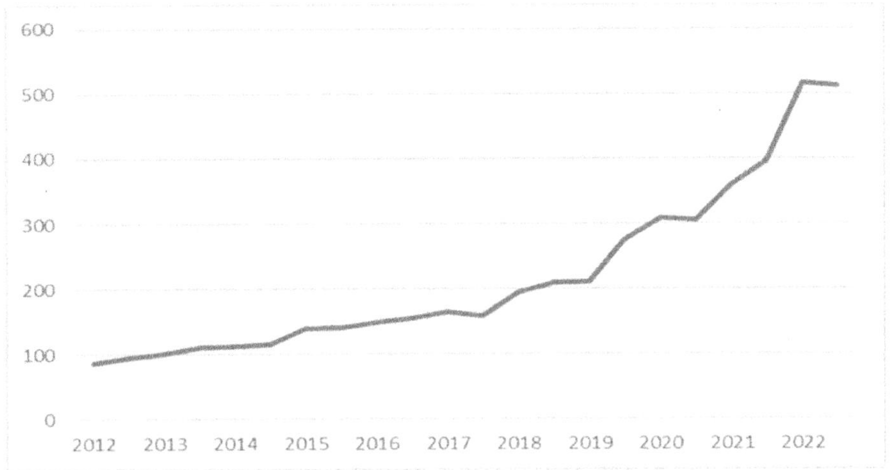

34.   D.R. HORTON INC.

WKN: 884312 ISIN: US23331A1097

Horton Circle 1341 76011 Arlington, TX, **USA**

Internet   http://www.drhorton.com

Company

D.R. HORTON INC. is a U.S. residential construction company. Its operations include home construction, financial services, leasing and other activities. The Company also provides financial services such as mortgage financing and title transfer to homebuyers and leases multifamily and single-family homes. In addition, the Company provides title services and acquires other residential construction companies.

Over the past ten years, D.R. HORTON has gained an average of **18% p.a.**, and 59% over the last 12 months.

D.R. HORTON INC. share chart (2012 - 2022) in euros

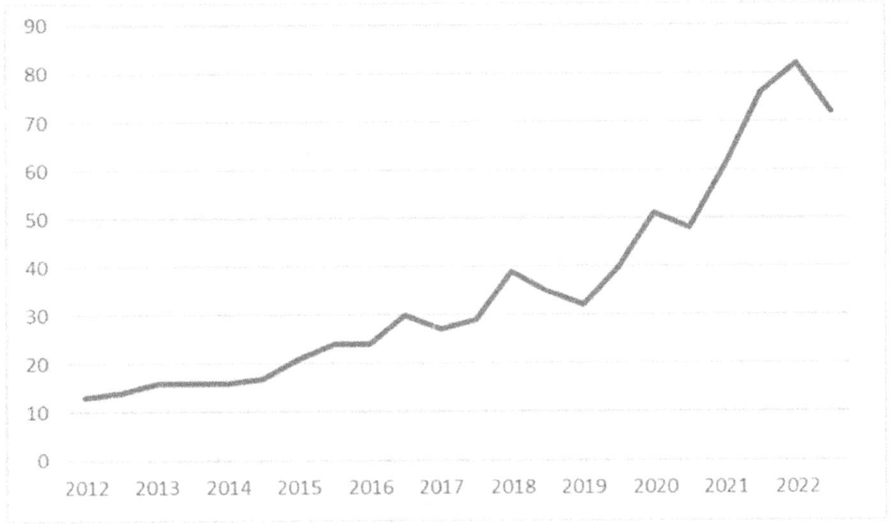

35.   ENTEGRIS INC.

WKN: 938201 ISIN: US29362U1043

129 Concord Road, Billerica, MA 01821 **USA**

Internet   https://www.entegris.com

Company

ENTEGRIS INC. helps manufacturers increase yields by improving contamination control in several key processes, including photolithography, wet etching and cleaning, chemical-mechanical planarization, thin film deposition, bulk chemical processing, wafer and reticle handling and shipping, and testing, assembly and packaging. Approximately 80% of the company's products are used in the semiconductor industry.

Over the past ten years, ENTEGRIS has gained an average of **33% p.a.**, and 60% over the last 12 months.

ENTEGRIS INC. share chart (2012 - 2022) in euros

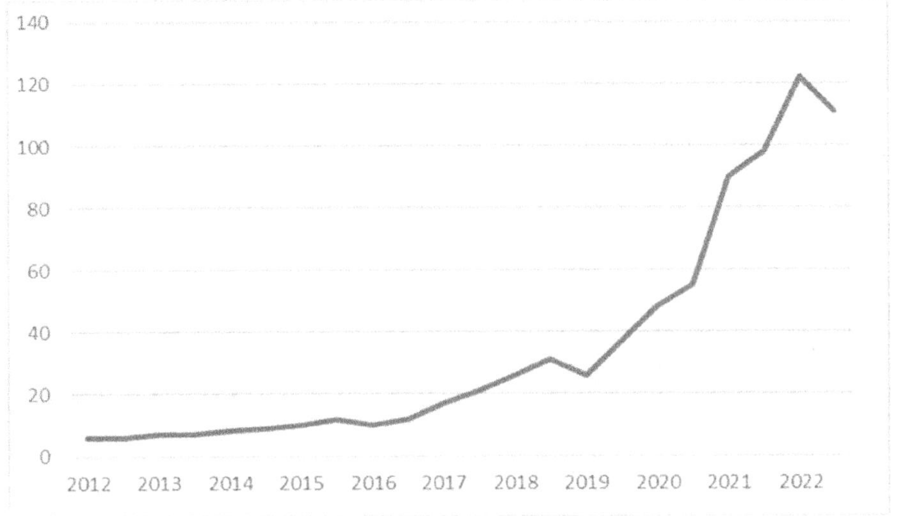

36.   HYPOPORT SE

WKN: 549336 **ISIN:** DE0005493365

Heidestraße 8 10557 Berlin, **GERMANY**

INTERNET   https://www.hypoport.com

Company

HYPOPORT SE is an internet-based financial services provider. HYPOPORT SE consists of a network of technology companies for the credit, real estate and insurance industries. The group distributes financial products through Dr. Klein & Co. AG and brokers financial products on a transaction platform on the internet.

Over the past ten years, HYPOPORT has gained an average of **33% p.a.**, and 40% over the last 12 months.

HYPOPORT SE share chart (2013 – 2023) in euros

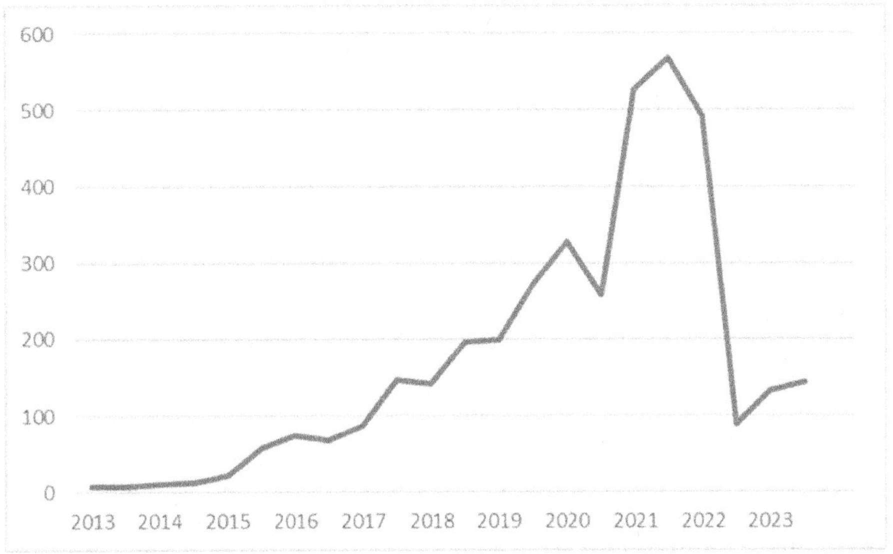

37. INTER PARFUMS INC.

WKN: 883617 **ISIN:** US4583341098

551 Fifth Avenue, New York, New York 10176, **USA**

INTERNET   https://www.interparfumsinc.com

Company

INTER PARFUMS INC. produces, markets and distributes high-quality perfumes and cosmetics for licensees Burberry, Van Cleef & Arpels, Jimmy Choo, Paul Smith, Montblanc, S.T. Dupont and Boucheron. The company operates in Europe and the United States. INTER PARFUMS INC. products are sold in over 100 countries worldwide.

Over the past decade, INTER PARFUMS has gained an average of **19% p.a.**, and 24% over the last 12 months.

INTER PARFUMS INC. share chart (2013 - 2023) in euros

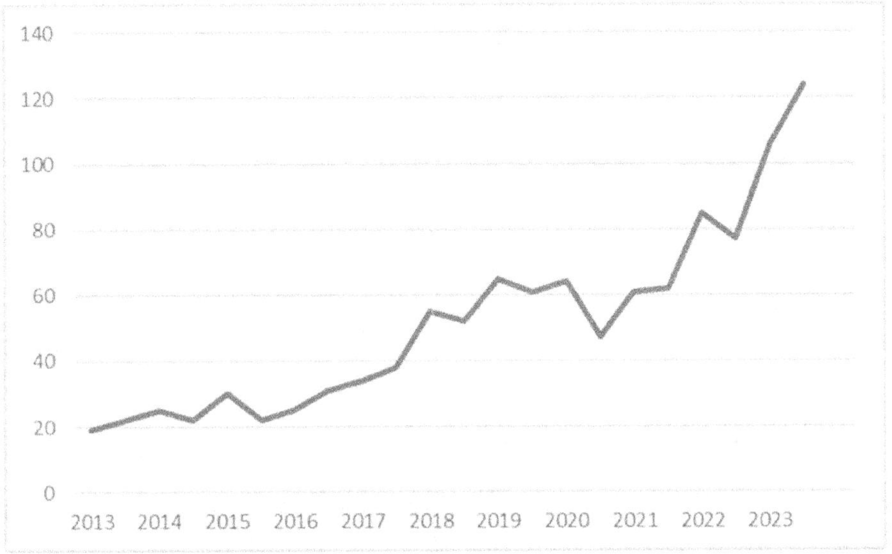

38.   KADANT INC.

WKN: 884567 ISIN: US48282T1043

One Technology Park Drive, Westford, MA 01886, **USA**

Internet   https://kadant.com

Company

KADANT INC. is one of the leading suppliers in the global pulp and paper industry. The Group offers various products and services for increasing efficiency and quality in pulp and paper production. The portfolio includes paper machine accessories and systems for stock preparation, liquids handling and water management. KADANT INC. products are used in the steel, rubber, plastics, food and textile industries. The company's products and services play an essential role in increasing efficiency, optimizing energy use and maximizing productivity in the process industry. At the same time, the company helps its customers drive their sustainability initiatives with products that reduce waste or generate more yield with fewer inputs, especially fibers, energy and water.

Over the past ten years, KADANT has gained an average of **25% p.a.**, and 50% over the last 12 months.

KADANT INC. share chart (2012 - 2022) in euros

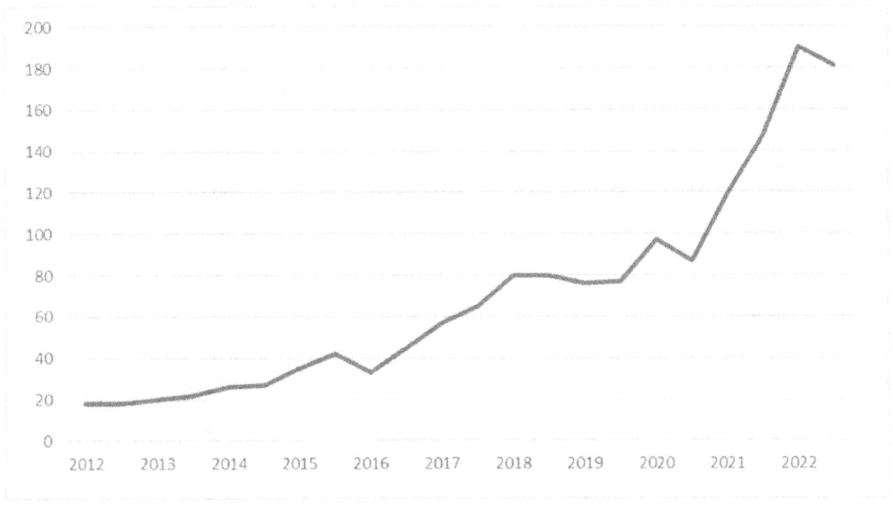

39.   KLA-TENCOR CORP.

WKN: 865884 ISIN: US4824801009

Technology Drive 1 95035 Milpitas, CA, **USA**

Internet   http://www.kla-tencor.com

Company

KLA-TENCOR CORP. is the world's leading process control and yield management company for the semiconductor and related microelectronics industries. The group offers a comprehensive portfolio of products spanning the entire production chain, from research to final product. The company's product areas include Chip Manufacturing, Wafer Manufacturing, Reticle Manufacturing, Data Storage Media/Head Manufacturing, Solar Manufacturing, High Brightness LED Manufacturing, Compound Semiconductor Manufacturing, MEMS Manufacturing, General Purpose, Labs, and Certified Used Equipment. The portfolio was created to help integrated circuit manufacturers manage their yields throughout the wafer manufacturing process, from R&D profit analysis to mass production.

Over the past ten years, KLA-TENCOR has gained an average of **26% p.a.**, and 68% over the last 12 months.

UNITEDHEALTH GROUP INC. share chart (2013 - 2023) in euros

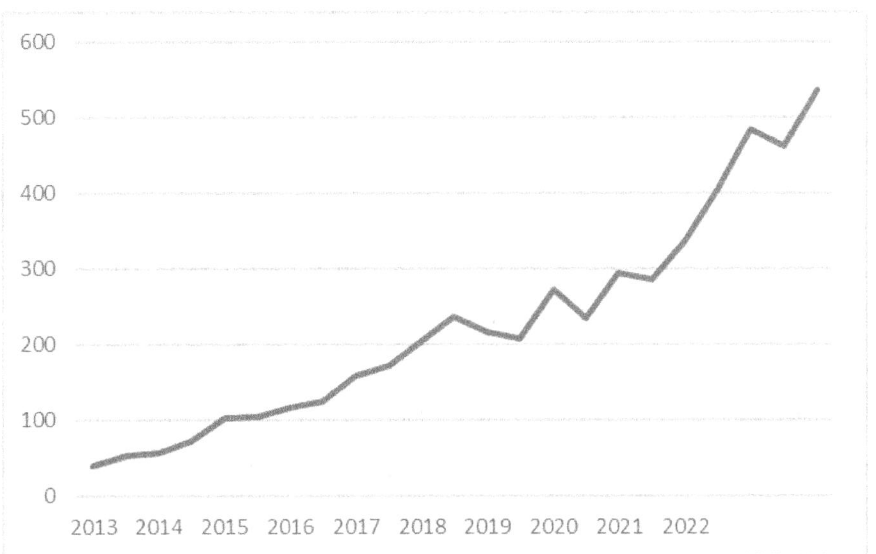

40.   LAM RESEARCH CORP.

WKN: 869686 ISIN: US5128071082

Cushing Parkway 4650 94538-6401 Fremont, CA, **USA**

Internet   http://www.lamresearch.com

Company

LAM RESEARCH CORP. is a leading supplier of wafer equipment and complementary services to the semiconductor industry and is a technological pioneer in the field of etch technology. In cooperation with various subsidiaries and affiliates, the company operates at production sites in North America, Europe and Asia. Furthermore, the company has subsidiaries in Austria, China, Japan, the Netherlands, Switzerland and the United Kingdom.

Over the past ten years, LAM RESEARCH has gained an average of **33% p.a.**, and 84% over the last 12 months.

LAM RESEARCH CORP. share chart (2012 - 2022) in euros

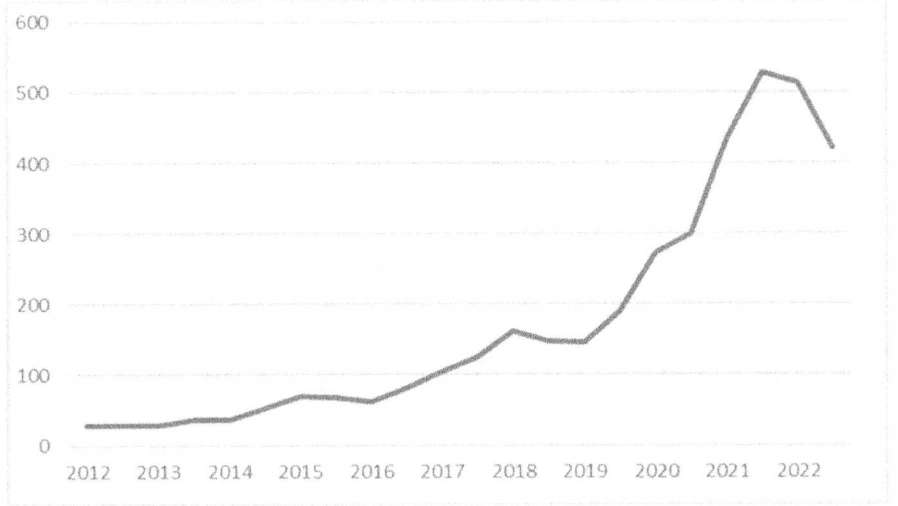

41.   LVMH MOET HENNESSY LOUIS VUITTON SE

WKN: 853292 **ISIN:** FR0000121014

Avenue Montaigne 22 75008 Paris, **FRANCE**

INTERNET   https://www.lvmh.com

Company

LVMH SE is a global manufacturer and distributor of luxury goods. The company today operates worldwide in its own stores in five areas of the luxury market: Wine & Spirits, Fashion & Leather Goods, Perfume & Cosmetics and Watches & Jewelry.

Over the past ten years, LVMH has gained an average of **22% p.a.**, and 9% over the last 12 months.

LVMH MOET HENNESSY LOUIS VUITTON SE share chart (2013 - 2023) in euros

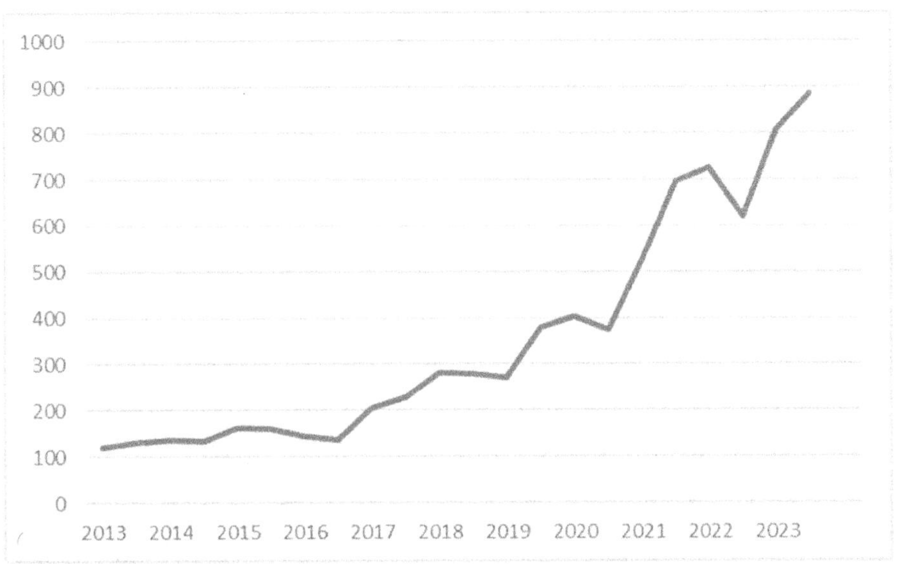

42.   MASCO CORP.

WKN: 856632 ISIN: US5745991068

College Parkway 17450 48152 Livonia, MI, **USA**

Internet   http://www.masco.com

Company

MASCO CORP. manufactures, distributes and installs home improvement and building products. The company manufactures a range of home improvement and building products, including faucets, cabinets, architectural coatings, and windows. Furthermore, the company offers services such as the installation of insulation and other materials.

Over the past ten years, MASCO has gained an average of **18% p.a.**, and 37% over the last 12 months.

MASCO CORP. share chart (2012 - 2022) in euros

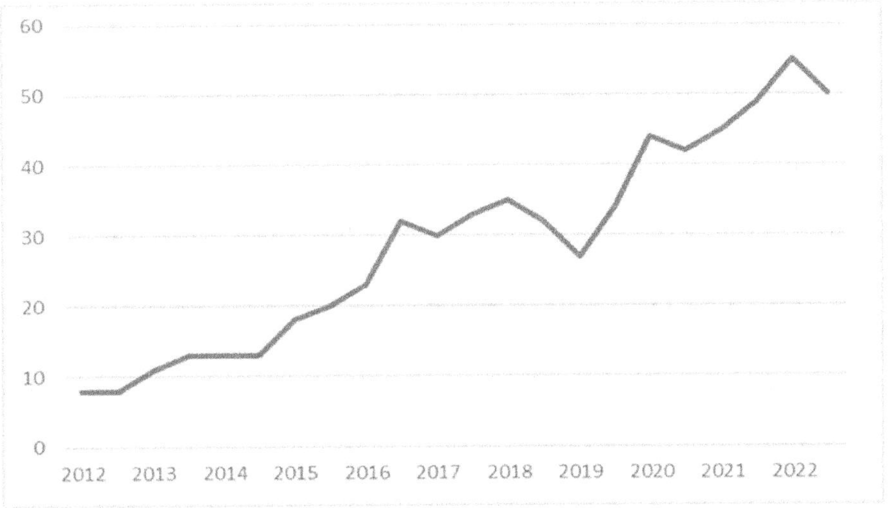

43.   MICROSOFT CORP.

WKN: 870747 ISIN: US5949181045

Microsoft Way 1 98052-6399 Redmond, WA, **USA**

Internet   http://www.microsoft.com

MICROSOFT CORP. share chart (2012 - 2022) in euros

Company

MICROSOFT CORP. is a leading global manufacturer of PC software. The company offers a wide range of software products and services for various user devices. The product range extends from Windows operating systems for PCs, mobile devices and networks, server software for client-server environments, application programs and desktop applications for companies as well as private users and multimedia applications to Internet platforms and developer tools. In addition to the online services Bing and MSN Portals, the portfolio also includes Skype and products and services related to the Xbox games console. In 2016, the LinkedIn Corporation was acquired. The Group is represented in more than 100 countries worldwide.

Over the past ten years, MICROSOFT has gained an average of **28% p.a.,** and 56% over the last 12 months.

MICROSOFT CORP. share chart (2012 - 2022) in euros

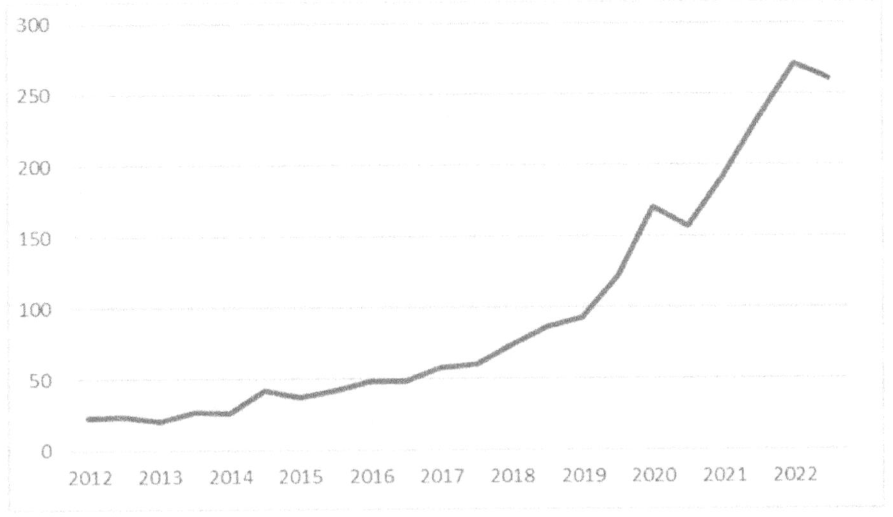

44.   MONCLER S.P.A.

WKN: A1W66W **ISIN**: IT0004965148

Via Enrico Stendhal, 47 20144 Milano, **ITALY**

INTERNET   https://www.monclergroup.com/

Company

MONCLER S.P.A. produces and sells men's, women's and children's clothing and corresponding accessories under the brand name Moncler. The company distributes its collections through 180 of its own boutiques, as well as through exclusive department stores and international fashion specialty stores.

Over the past ten years, MONCLER has gained an average of **18% p.a.**, and 11% over the last 12 months.

MONCLER S.P.A. share chart (2014 - 2023) in euros

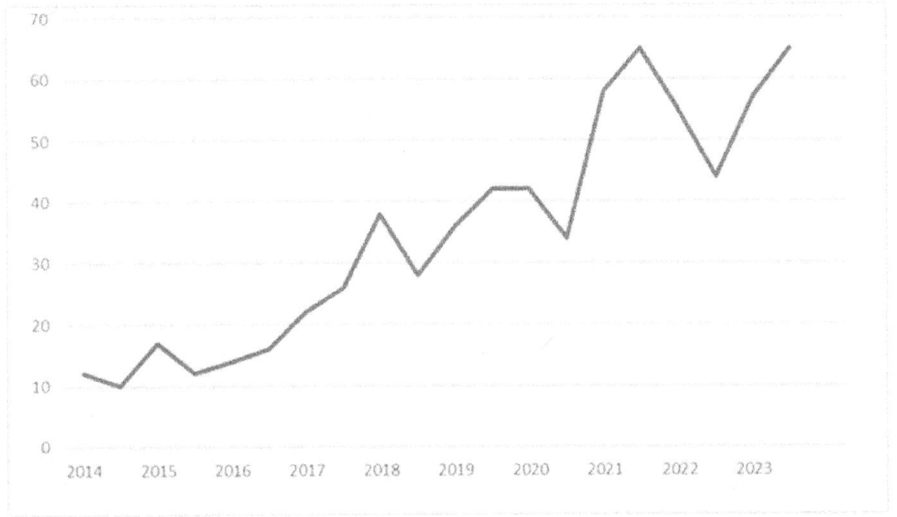

45.   MONOLITHIC POWER SYSTEMS INC.

WKN: A0DLC4 ISIN: US6098391054

5808 Lake Washington Blvd., WA 98033, **USA**

Internet   https://www.monolithicpower.com

Company

MONOLITHIC POWER SYSTEMS INC. provides integrated circuits for systems used in cloud computing, telecommunications infrastructure, automotive, industrial and consumer applications. Products are distributed through third-party vendors, value-added resellers and directly to original equipment manufacturers, original design manufacturers and electronics manufacturing service providers in China, Taiwan, Europe, Korea, Southeast Asia, Japan and the United States.

Over the past ten years, MONOLITHIC POWER SYSTEMS has gained an average of **39% p.a.,** and 44% over the last 12 months.

MONOLITHIC POWER SYSTEMS INC. share chart (2012 - 2022) in euros

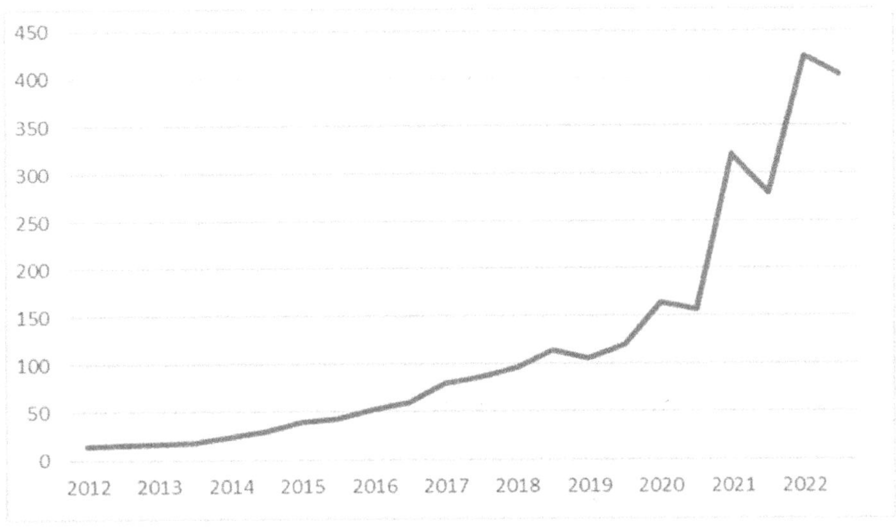

46.   NETFLIX INC.

WKN: 552484 **ISIN:** US64110L1061

Winchester Circle 100 95032 Los Gatos, CA, **USA**

INTERNET   https://ir.netflix.net

Company

NETFLIX INC. offers entertainment services and is one of the world's leading providers in this field with its portfolio of TV series and films. The company has around 231 million paying members in 190 countries. Licenses for the available formats are acquired from production and distribution companies and then made available to customers. Netflix also produces many of the formats on offer itself.

Over the past ten years, NETFLIX has gained an average of **25% p.a.,** and 80% over the last 12 months.

NETFLIX INC. share chart (2013 - 2023) in euros

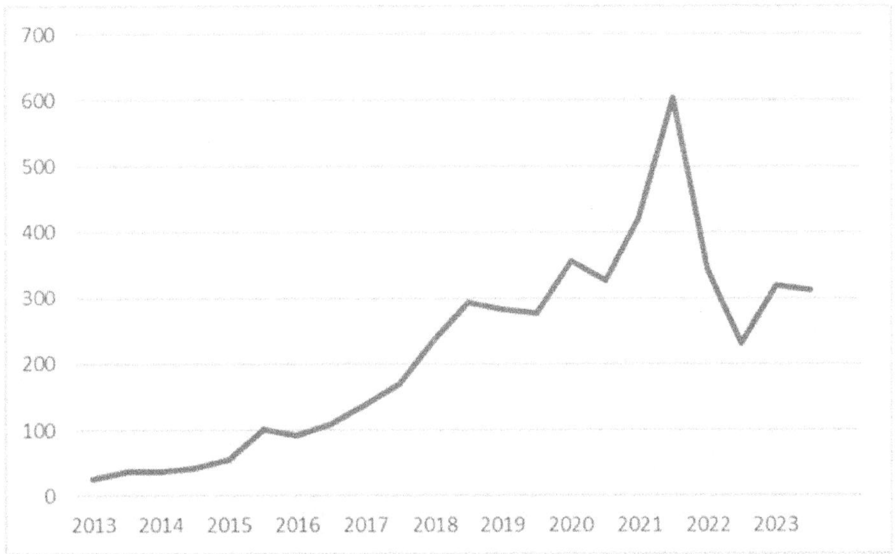

47.   NOVA MEASURING INSTRUMENTS LTD.

WKN: 937092 ISIN: IL0010845571

7610201 Rehovot, **Israel**

Internet   http://www.nova.co.il

Company

NOVA MEASURING INSTRUMENTS LTD. is a leading innovator and major provider of metrology solutions for advanced process control in semiconductor manufacturing. The company solicits high-performance metrology products combined with high-precision hardware and software to deliver a leading-edge portfolio of solutions for the semiconductor industry. Nova is represented worldwide through offices in Israel, Taiwan, Korea, Singapore, China, USA, Japan and Europe.

Over the past ten years, NOVA MEASURING INSTRUMENTS has gained an average of **32% p.a.**, and 78% over the last 12 months.

NOVA MEASURING INSTRUMENTS LTD. share chart (2017 - 2022) in euros

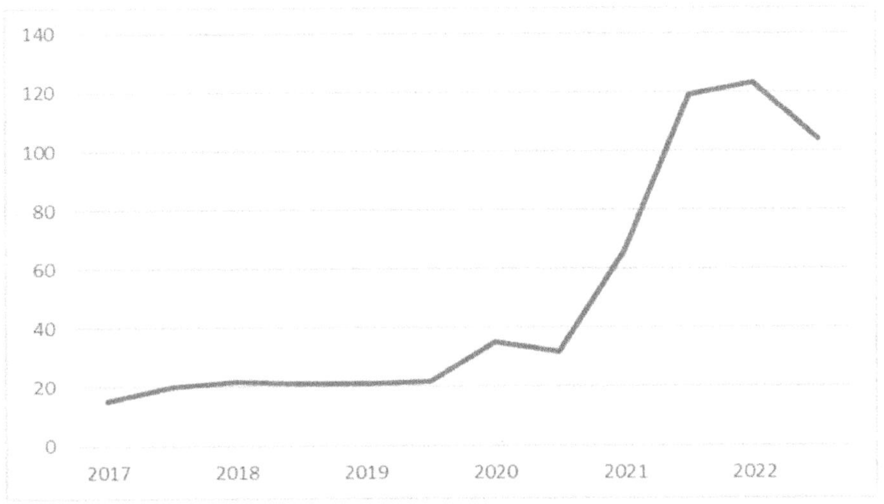

48.   NVIDIA CORP.

WKN: 918422 ISIN: US67066G1040

San Tomas Expressway 2788 95051 Santa Clara, CA, **USA**

Internet   http://www.nvidia.com

Company

NVIDIA CORP. is a multinational technology company and leading manufacturer of IT hardware. Its main customers are in the gaming, mobile computing and automotive sectors. The company designs, develops and markets graphics and media communications processors and related software for PCs, workstations and digital entertainment platforms, and manufactures a variety of 3D graphics processors as well as graphics processing units (GPUs) used in desktop PCs, smartphones, tablets and laptops. NVIDIA CORP. markets its products worldwide.

Over the past ten years, NVIDIA has gained an average of **58% p.a.**, and 222% over the last 12 months.

NVIDIA CORP. share chart (2012 - 2022) in euros

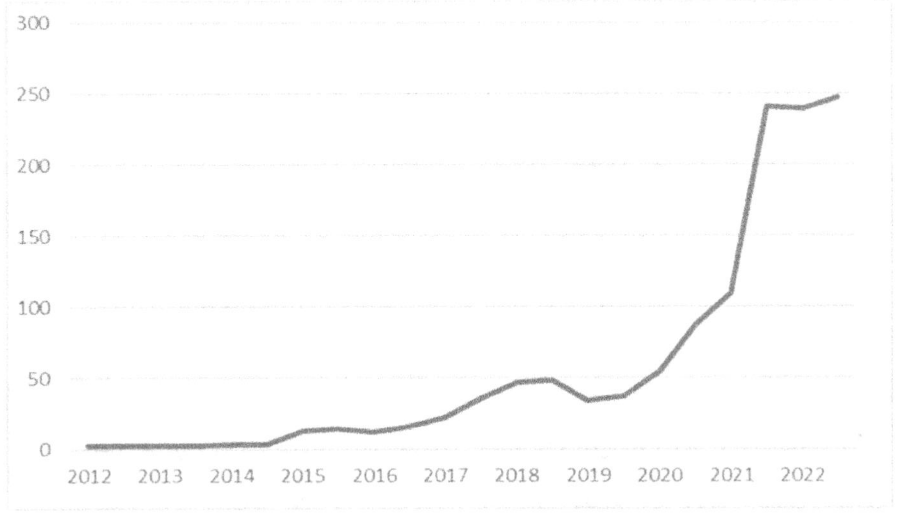

49.   PALO ALTO NETWORKS INC.

WKN: A1JZ0Q ISIN: US6974351057

3000 Tannery Way Santa Clara, California 95054, **USA**

Internet   http://www.paloaltonetworks.com7

Company

PALO ALTO NETWORKS INC. is a provider of cybersecurity solutions. The company's platform is primarily focused on enterprise customers and combines security, automation and analytics. The company's services are applied to clouds, networks and mobile devices.

Over the past ten years, PALO ALTO NETWORKS has gained an average of **28% p.a.**, and 44% over the last 12 months.

PALO ALTO NETWORKS INC. share chart (2012 - 2022) in euros

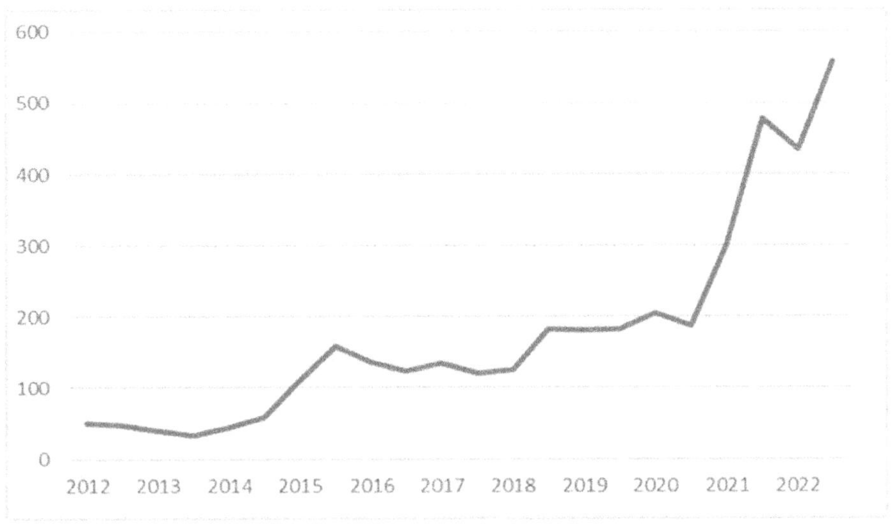

50.   PROCTER & GAMBLE CO

WKN: 852062 **ISIN:** US7427181091

Procter & Gamble Plaza 1 45202 Cincinnati, OH , **USA**

INTERNET   https://us.pg.com/

Company

PROCTER & GAMBLE CO is a manufacturer of consumer goods for everyday use. The product spectrum includes several hundred brands and product variations, ranging from beauty, hygiene and health to household and hairdressing products and pet food. The product range is distributed through bulk buyers, grocery stores and drugstores, as well as smaller retail outlets.

Over the past ten years, PROCTER & GAMBLE has gained an average of **10% p.a.**, and 14% over the last 12 months.

PROCTER & GAMBLE CO share chart (2013 - 2023) in euros

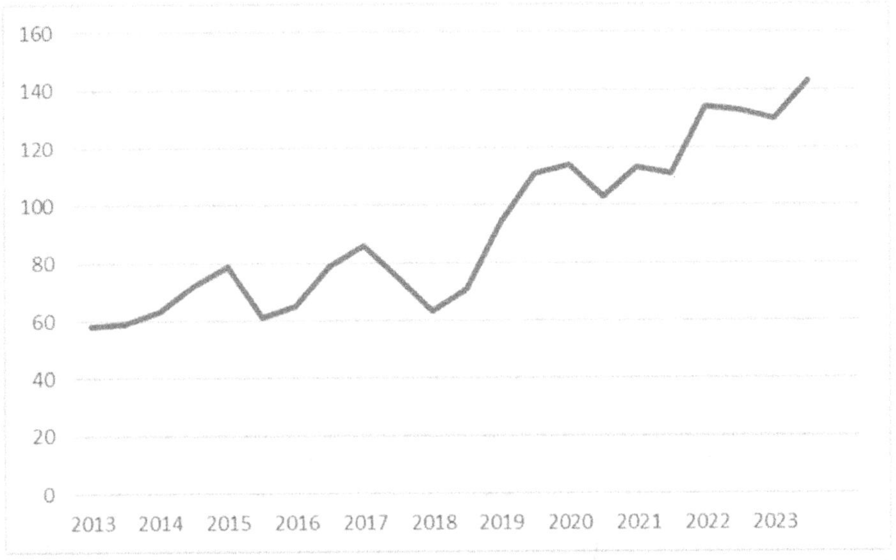

51.   PROGRESSIVE CORP.

WKN: 865496 ISIN: US7433151039

Wilson Mills Road 6300 44143 Mayfield Village, OH, **USA**

Internet   http://www.progressive.com

Company

PROGRESSIVE CORP. is an insurance holding company. The company provides personal auto insurance, commercial auto and truck insurance, and other property specialty insurance and related services. The company's portfolio primarily serves personal lines and small commercial customers.

Over the past ten years, PROGRESSIVE has gained an average of **20% p.a.**, and 31% over the last 12 months.

PROGRESSIVE CORP. share chart (2012 - 2022) in euros

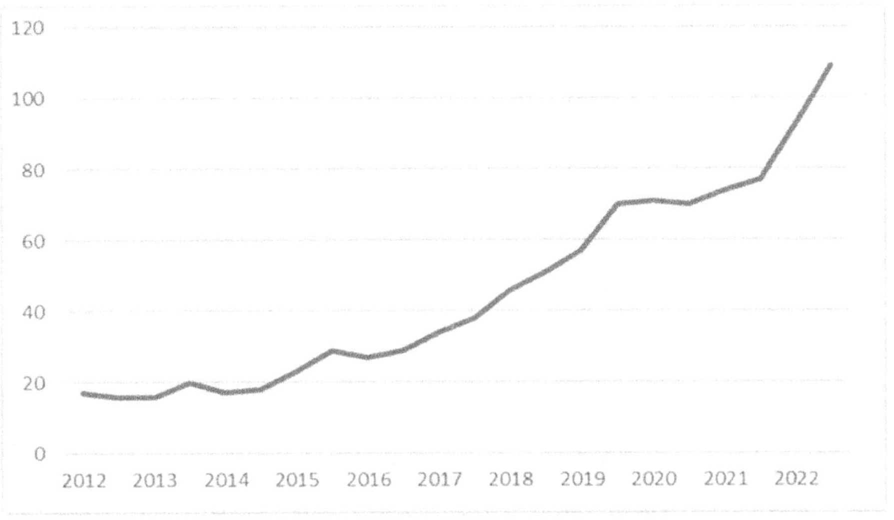

52.   QUANTA SERVICES INC.

WKN: 912294 ISIN: US74762E1029

Post Oak Blvd. 1360 77056 Houston, Texas, **USA**

Internet   http://www.quantaservices.com

Company

QUANTA SERVICES INC. is a leading provider of contract services, offering infrastructure solutions primarily to utility and oil and natural gas companies. The services offered include the design, installation, expansion, repair and maintenance of energy infrastructures. QUANTA SERVICES INC. operates primarily in the USA, Canada and Australia.

Over the past ten years, QUANTA SERVICES has gained an average of **20% p.a.**, and 38% over the last 12 months.

QUANTA SERVICES INC. share chart (2012 - 2022) in US dollars

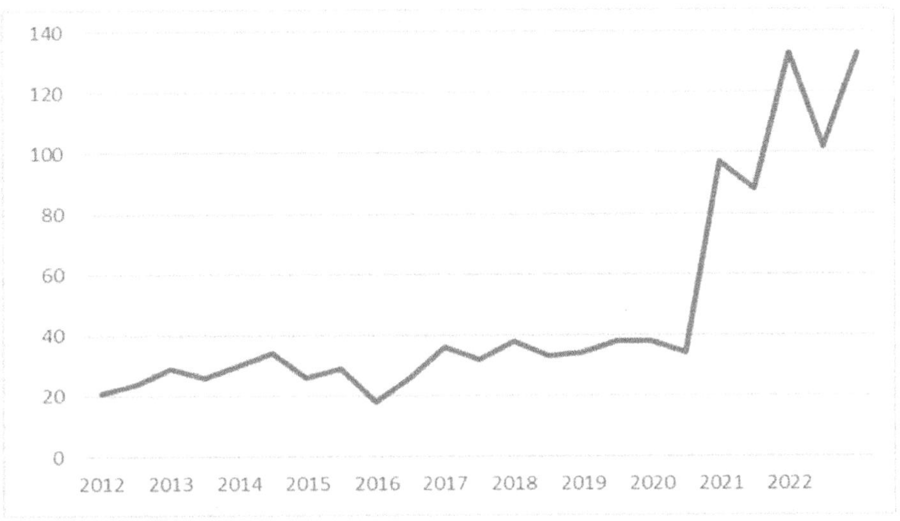

53.   RECORDATI INDUSTRIA CHIMICA E FARMACEUTICA SPA

WKN: A0EABR ISIN: IT0003828271

Via Matteo Civitali 1 IT-20148 Mailand, **Italy**

Internet   http://www.recordati.it

Company

RECORDATI SPA is an internationally oriented pharmaceutical group. The Group researches, develops, manufactures and markets drugs for the primary care and drugs for the treatment of diseases. RECORDATI SPA markets both proprietary and licensed drugs for many therapeutic areas. The company is focused on new specialties in genitourinary therapy and the treatment of rare diseases. Subsidiaries are located in major European countries, Turkey, North Africa, and the United States.

Over the past ten years, RECORDATI has gained an average of **22% p.a.**, and 30% over the last 12 months.

RECORDATI SPA share chart (2012 - 2022) in euros

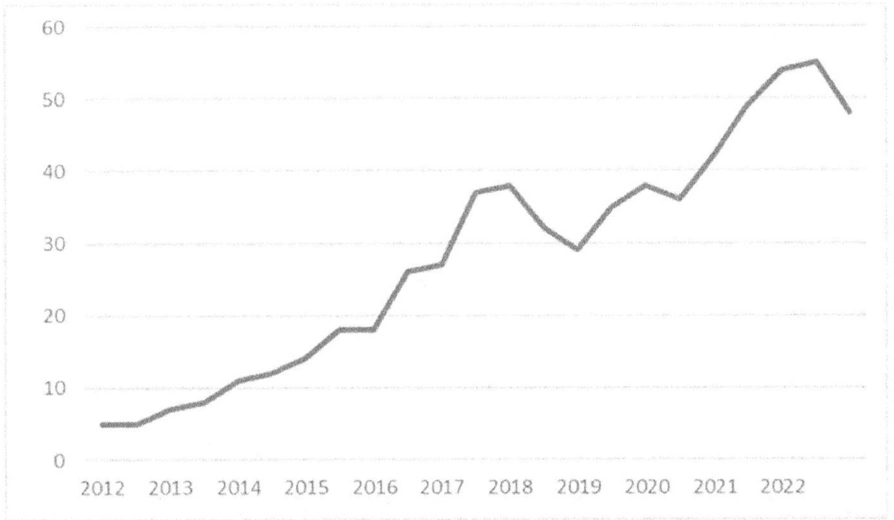

54.   REPUBLIC SERVICES INC.

WKN: 915201 ISIN: US7607591002

SouthEast Sixth Street 110 33301 Fort Lauderdale, FL, **USA**

Internet   http://www.republicservices.com

Company

REPUBLIC SERVICES INC. is a waste management company and the second largest provider of non-hazardous solid waste environmental services in the United States. In addition to a fleet of refuse trucks, REPUBLIC SERVICES INC. owns or operates 192 transfer stations, 192 landfills and 64 recycling centers. The company also operates more than 71 landfill gas and renewable energy projects and disposes of household and industrial waste for commercial, industrial, municipal and residential customers.

Over the past ten years, REPUBLIC SERVICES has gained an average of **19% p.a.**, and 37% over the last 12 months.

REPUBLIC SERVICES INC. share chart (2012 - 2022) in euros

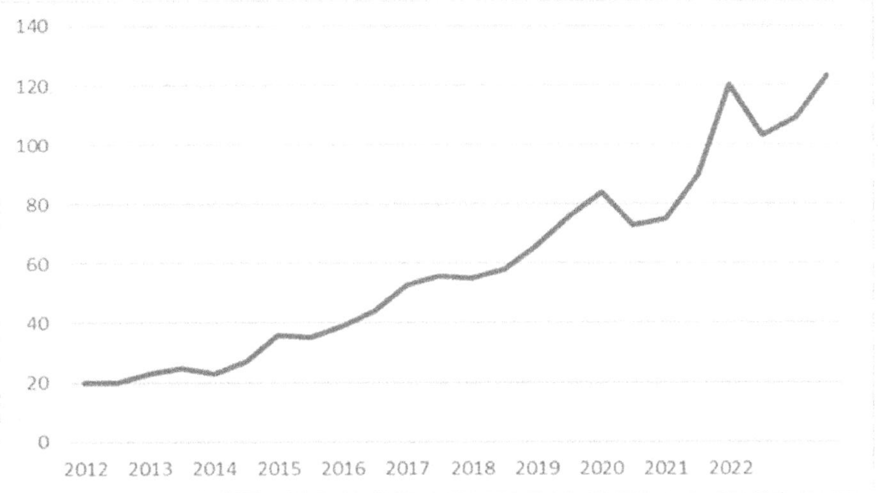

55.   ROPER TECHNOLOGIES INC.

WKN: 883563 ISIN: US7766961061

Professional Parkway East 6901, Suite 200 34240 Sarasota,
FL, **USA**

Internet   http://www.roperind.com

Company

ROPER TECHNOLOGIES INC is a diversified technology
company, provider of technical products and service
solutions for end markets in various industries, such as the
water, energy, transportation, education or healthcare
industries. ROPER TECHNOLOGIES INC is focused on
individual markets, producing solutions for the oil and gas
industry, the computer industry, or developing specialized
imaging processes for medical technology, for example.
ROPER TECHNOLOGIES INC operates mainly within the USA,
but is active in Europe, Asia and South America.

Over the past ten years, ROPER TECHNOLOGIES has gained
an average of **18% p.a.**, and 26% over the last 12 months.

ROPER TECHNOLOGIES INC. share chart (2012 - 2022) in euros

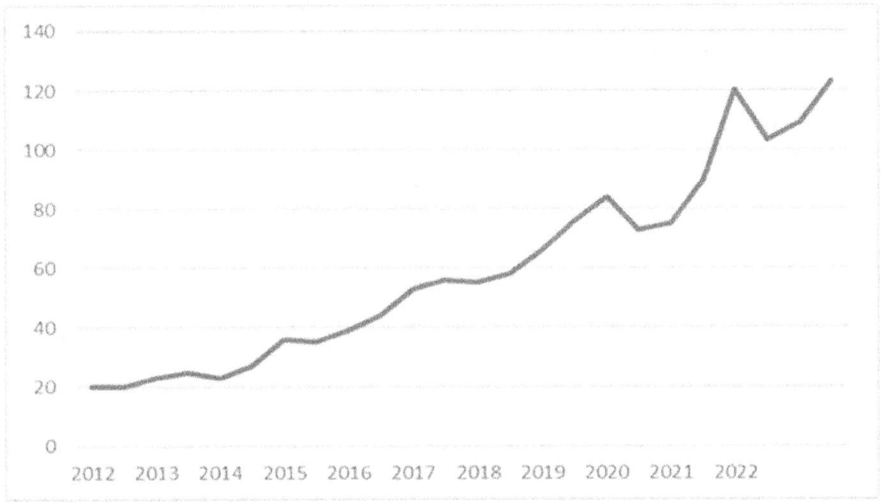

56.　SAFRAN SA

WKN: 924781 **ISIN:** FR0000073272

Boulevard du Général-Martial-Valin 2 75724, Paris Cedex 15, **FRANCE**

INTERNET　https://www.safran-group.com/

Company

SAFRAN SA is a technology company. SAFRAN SA, together with its subsidiaries, is active worldwide in the aerospace and defense sectors. The company's business activities are divided into aerospace, space and defense. The company's products and services are used in civil and military aircraft and helicopters.

.

Over the past ten years, SAFRAN has gained an average of **12% p.a.**, and 46% over the last 12 months.

SAFRAN SA share chart (2013- 2023) in euros

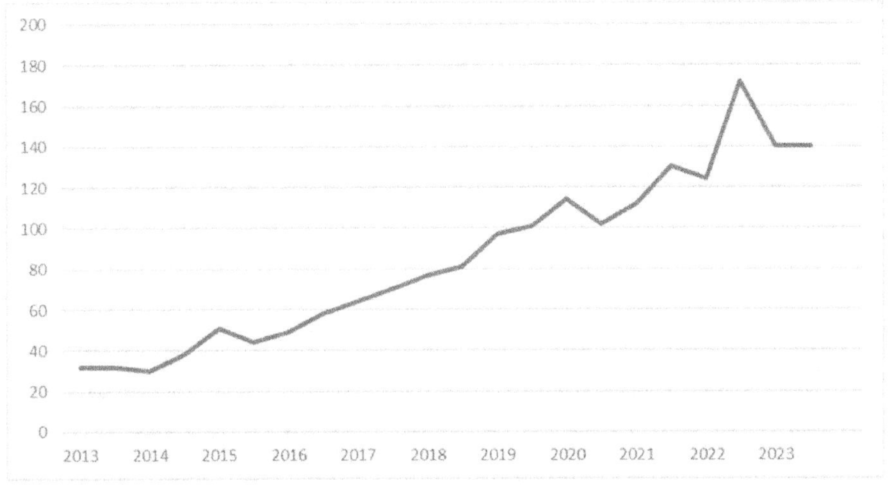

57.   SHERWIN WILLIAMS CO.

WKN: 856050 ISIN: US8243481061

Prospect Avenue NorthWest 101 44115 Cleveland, Ohio, **USA**

Internet   http://www.sherwin-williams.co

Company

SHERWIN WILLIAMS CO. is a leader in the manufacture, distribution and sale of coatings and related products. Its product portfolio includes architectural coatings, industrial coatings and related products. The company also operates numerous specialty stores in nearly every U.S. state, Canada and some Latin American countries

Over the past ten years, SHERWIN WILLIAMS has gained an average of **22% p.a.**, and 37% over the last 12 months.

SHERWIN WILLIAMS CO. share chart (2012 - 2022) in euros

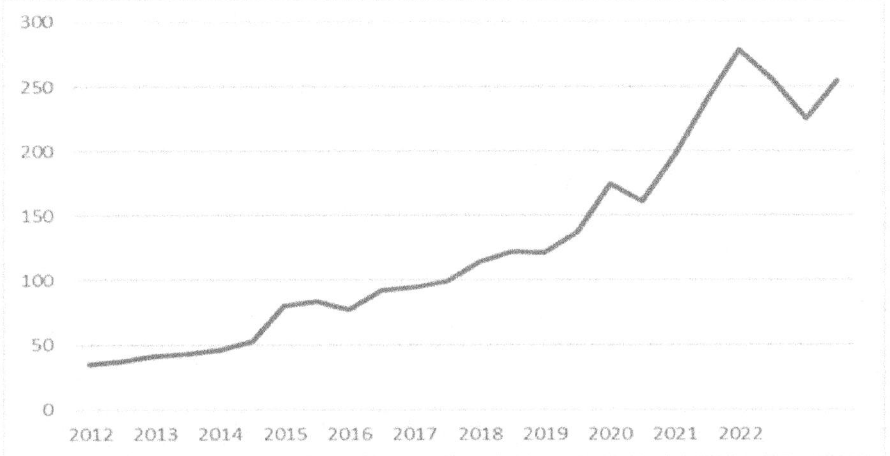

58.   STRYKER CORP.

WKN: 864952 ISIN: US8636671013

AIRVIEW BOULEVARD 2825 49002 KALAMAZOO, MI, **USA**

INTERNET   HTTP://WWW.STRYKER.COM

Company

STRYKER CORP. is one of the world's leading suppliers of medical and surgical products. Its products include orthopedic implants, trauma systems, osteogenic protein-1 responsible for bone growth, various surgical instruments, endoscopy systems, and various accessories and consumables for patient care. In the United States, most of these products are marketed directly to physicians, hospitals and other healthcare facilities. Internationally, the products are sold in over 100 countries around the world.

Over the past decade, STRYKER gained **17% p.a.** on average, and 31% over the last 12 months.

STRYKER CORP. share chart (2012 - 2022) in euros

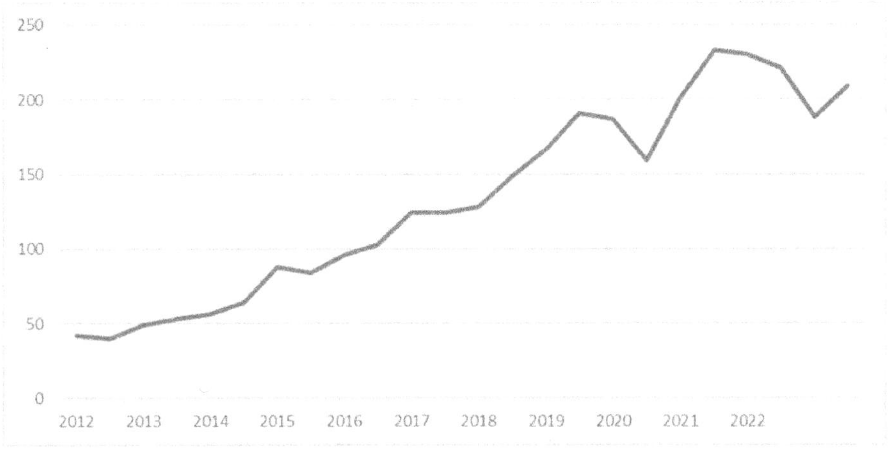

59.   SWISS LIFE HOLDING AG

WKN: 778237 ISIN: CH0014852781

GENERAL GUISAN-QUAI 40 8022 ZÜRICH, **SWITZERLAND**

INTERNET   HTTP://WWW.SWISSLIFE.COM

Company

SWISS LIFE HOLDING AG is a leading European provider of comprehensive life insurance, pension and financial solutions. SWISS LIFE HOLDING AG operates in the core markets of Switzerland, France and Germany as well as in cross-border business from Liechtenstein, Luxembourg, Singapore and Dubai.

In the past ten years, SWISS LIFE has gained **19% p.a.** on average, and 28% over the last 12 months.

SWISS LIFE HOLDING AG share chart (2012 – 2022) in euros

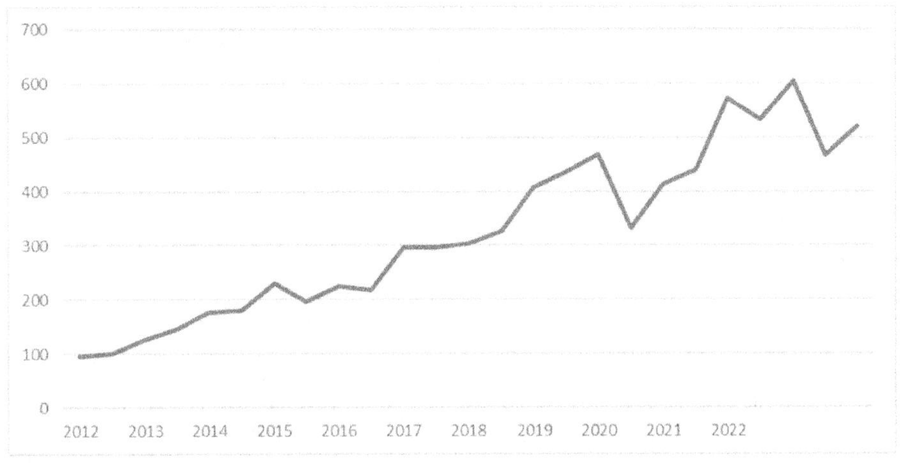

60.   SWISSQUOTE GROUP HOLDING SA

WKN: 938312 ISIN: CH0010675863

CHEMIN DE LA CRÉTAUX 33 1196 GLAND, **SWITZERLAND**

INTERNET   HTTP://WWW.SWISSQUOTE.CH

Company

SWISSQUOTE GROUP HOLDING SA is the parent company of a group that is the leading provider of online trading services and financial services for the financial and trading sector in Switzerland. The group includes Swissquote Bank SA and the Swissport financial portal. The retail business is complemented by securities and foreign exchange trading. SWISSQUOTE GROUP HOLDING SA distributes various credit cards of choice.

In the past ten years, SWISSQUOTE GROUP has gained **15% p.a.** on average, and 33% over the last 12 months.

SWISSQUOTE GROUP HOLDING SA share chart (2012 - 2022) in swiss franc

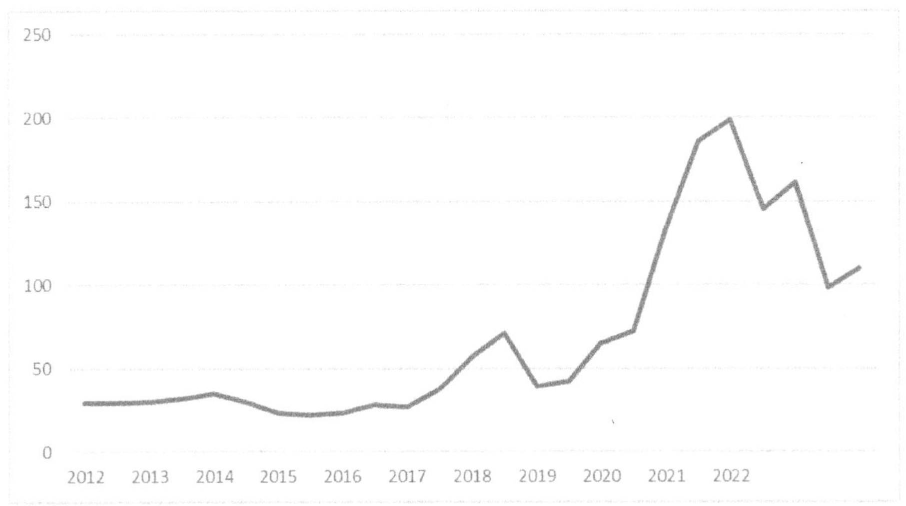

61.   SYNOPSYS INC.

WKN: 883703 ISIN: US8716071076

EAST MIDDLEFIELD ROAD 690 CA 94043 MOUNTAIN VIEW, CA, **USA**

INTERNET   HTTP://WWW.SYNOPSYS.COM

Company

SYNOPSYS INC. is a US-based leading software company. The company is a provider of electronic design automation software. Its products are used by designers of integrated circuits, for electronic products such as cell phones, computers and Internet routers. SYNOPSYS INC. also provides support services and training.

Over the past ten years, SYNOPSYS has gained an average of **32% p.a.**, and 63% over the last 12 months.

SYNOPSYS INC. share chart (2012 - 2022) in euros

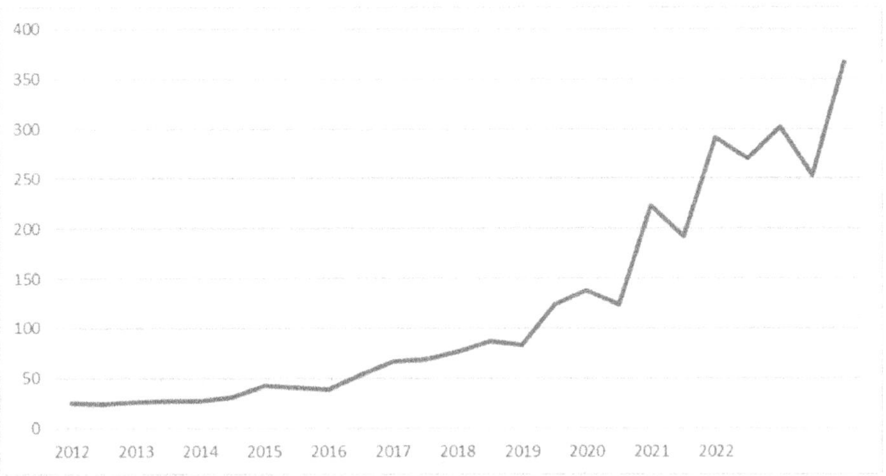

62.   TERUMO CORP.

WKN: 867003 ISIN: JP3546800008

2-44-1 HATAGAYA, SHIBUYA-KU, TOKYO 151-0072, **JAPAN**

INTERNET   HTTP://WWW.TERUMO.COM

Company

TERUMO CORP. manufactures and distributes medical products and equipment. The product range includes medical devices and accessories for use in hospitals, equipment for operating rooms, and special devices for the preparation and use of blood transfusions. Currently, TERUMO CORP. includes three companies and eight businesses that operate in over 160 countries and regions around the world.

Over the past ten years, TERUMO has gained an average of **15% p.a.,** and 39% over the last 12 months.

TERUMO CORP. share chart (2012 - 2022) in euros

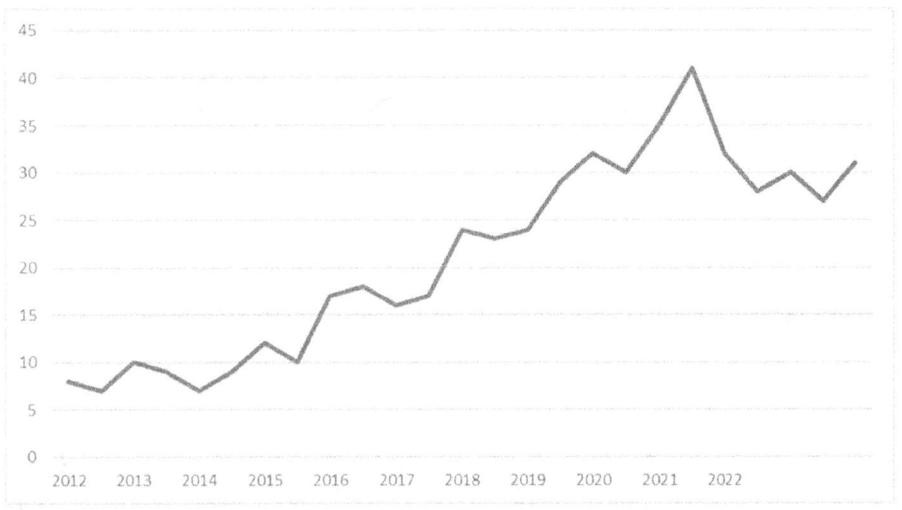

63.   TJX COMPANIES INC.

WKN: 854854 ISIN: US8725401090

COCHITUATE ROAD 770 01701 FRAMINGHAM, MA, **USA**

INTERNET   HTTP://WWW.TJX.COM

Company

TJX COMPANIES INC. is a U.S. retailer dealing in off-price apparel and home furnishings in the United States and worldwide. In Europe, the company is represented by the T.K. Maxx and HomeSense brands. The assortment consists of a mix of apparel, accessories, gifts and home goods.

Over the past ten years, TJX COMPANIES has gained an average of **13% p.a.**, and 26% over the last 12 months.

TJX COMPANIES INC. share chart (2012 – 2022) in euros

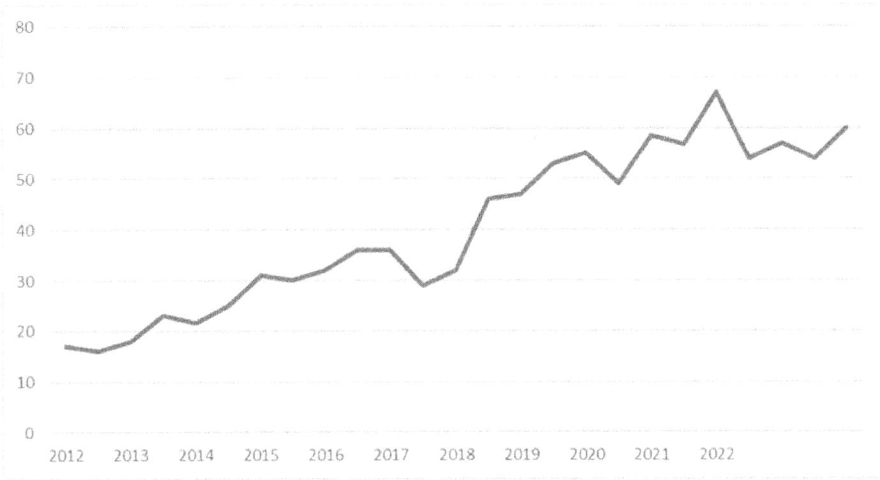

64.   T-MOBILE US INC.

WKN: A0MMP1 ISIN: US11133T1034

SE 38TH STREET 12920 98006 BELLEVUE, WASHINGTON,
USA

INTERNET   HTTP://WWW.T-MOBILE.COM

Company

T-MOBILE US INC. is one of the fastest growing mobile communications companies in the U.S. The company sells mobile communications services to more than 63 million customers in the postpaid, prepaid and wholesale segments. T-MOBILE US INC. also offers a portfolio of cell phones, tablets and other devices for mobile network access, as well as accessories such as headsets, headsets and cell phone accessories.

Over the past decade, T-MOBILE US has gained an average of **28% p.a.**, and 12% over the last 12 months.

T-MOBILE US INC. share chart (2012 - 2022) in euros

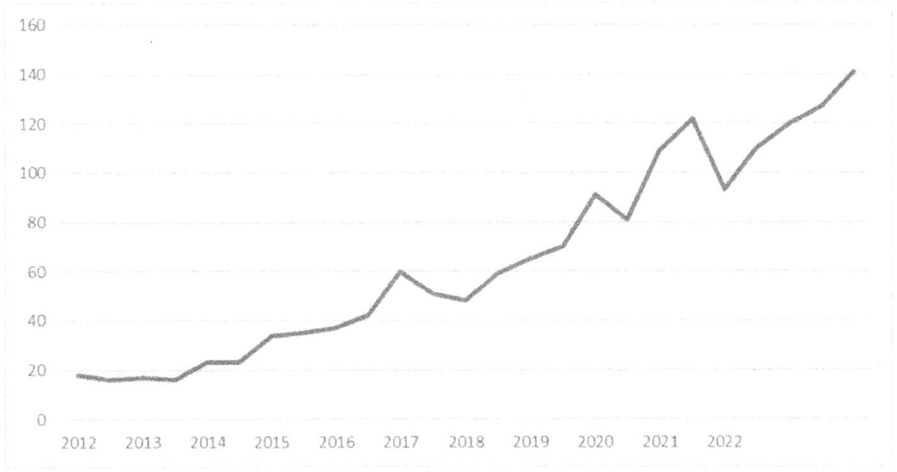

65.   TOPBUILD CORP.

WKN: A14UY4 ISIN: US89055F1030

475 North Williamson Boulevard, 32114 Daytona Beach,
USA

INTERNET   HTTP://WWW.TOPBUILD.COM

Company

TOPBUILD CORP. is an installation and distribution company of insulation and building materials for the construction industry, with approximately 235 locations throughout the United States. In addition to insulation materials and accessories, TOPBUILD CORP. also sells rain gutters, chimneys, closet shelving and roofing materials, among other products.

Over the past ten years, TOPBUILD has gained an average of **35% p.a.**, and 93% over the last 12 months.

TOPBUILD CORP. share chart (2017 - 2022) in euros

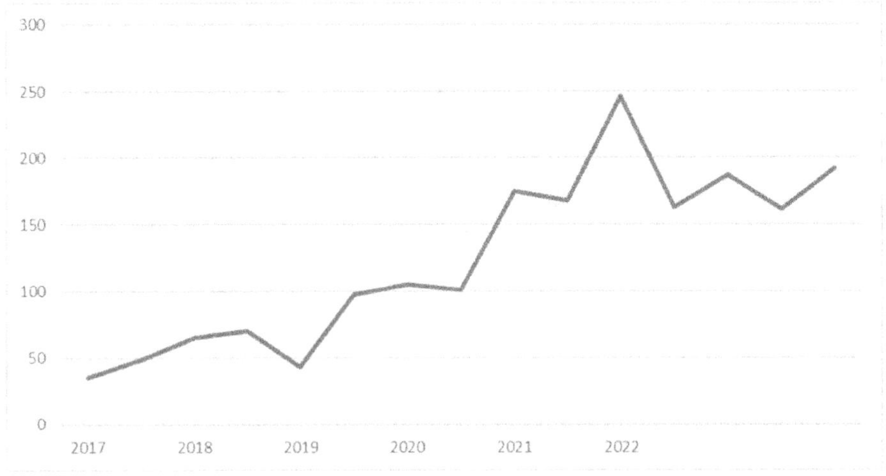

66.   TRANE TECHNOLOGIES PLC

WKN: A2P09K ISIN: IE00BK9ZQ967

170/175 LAKEVIEW DR. AIRSIDE BUSINESS PARK, SWORDS
CO. DUBLIN, **IRELAND**

INTERNET   HTTPS://WWW.TRANETECHNOLOGIES.COM/

Company

TRANE TECHNOLOGIES PLC is a diversified industrial company. The company operates in the fields of climate control systems, industrial and infrastructure solutions, and safety and security. TRANE TECHNOLOGIES PLC's product range includes, for example, air compressors, hardware for construction, microturbines, temperature control and cooling systems, tools, pumps and material handling systems, and safety systems for commercial and residential applications.

Over the past six years, TRANE TECHNOLOGIES has gained an average of **20% p.a.**, and 52% over the last 12 months.

TRANE TECHNOLOGIES PLC (2012 - 2022) in euros

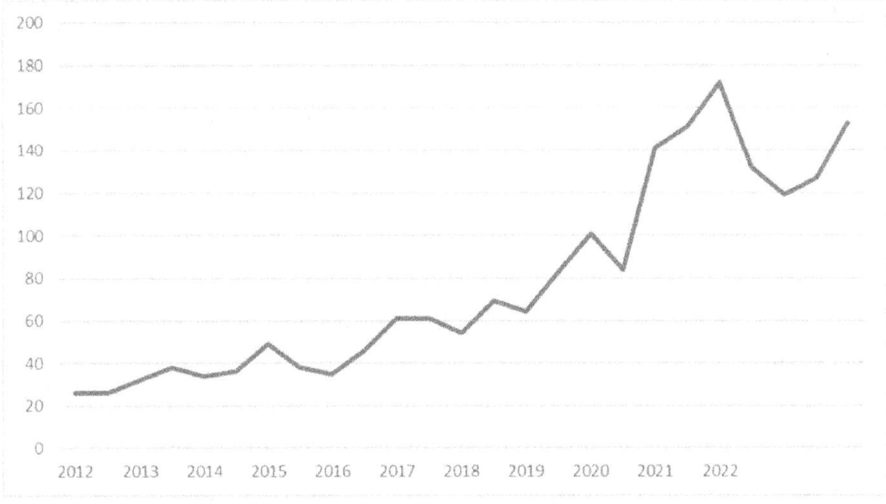

67.   TRANSDIGM GROUP INC.

WKN: A0JEP3 ISIN: US8936411003

1301 EAST 9TH STREET, SUITE 3000, CLEVELAND, OHIO
44114, **USA**

INTERNET   HTTP://WWW.TRANSDIGM.COM

Company

TRANSDIGM GROUP INC. is a worldwide designer,
manufacturer and supplier of advanced aircraft
components for use in virtually all commercial and military
aircraft. TRANSDIGM GROUP INC. offerings include
mechanical/electromechanical actuators and controls,
ignition systems, engine technology, and specialty pumps,
as well as cockpit safety components and systems,
specialized cockpit displays, audio systems, seat belts, and
lighting.

Over the past ten years, TRANSDIGM GROUP has gained an
average of **19% p.a.**, and 58% over the last 12 months.

TRANSDIGM GROUP INC. share chart (2012 - 2022) in euros

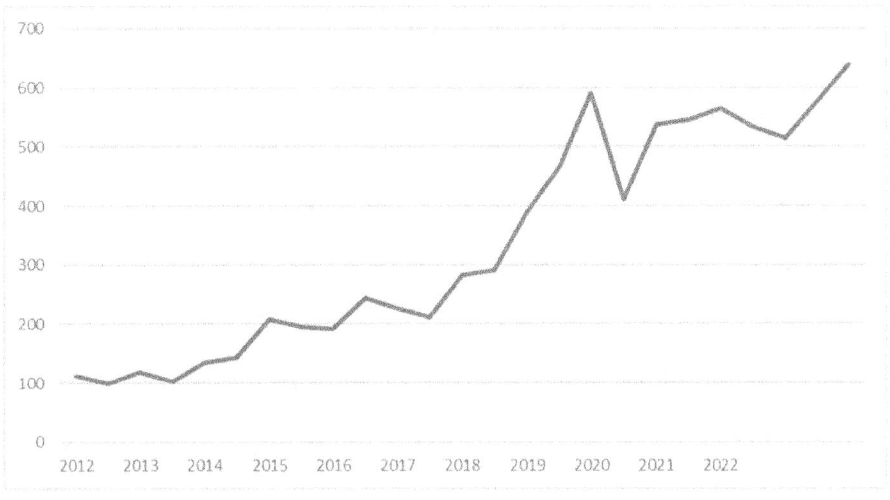

68. TREX COMPANY INC.

WKN: 938716 ISIN: US89531P1057

Bryan Fairbanks 160 Exeter Drive, Winchester, Virginia 22603-8605, **USA**

INTERNET HTTP://WWW.TREX.COM

Company

TREX COMPANY INC. is a major manufacturer of wood-alternative composite decking, railing, and other outdoor items made from recycled materials. Their manufacturing process combines recycled plastic film, like grocery bags and dry cleaning wrap, with reclaimed wood, some of which is swept from the floors of furniture factories. To procure the amount of plastic film necessary for production, TREX COMPANY INC. leans on partnerships with grocery store chains. The company's products are sold in over 6,700 outlets worldwide.

Over the past nine years, TREX has gained an average of **32% p.a.**, and 85% over the last 12 months.

TREX COMPANY INC. share chart (2012 - 2022) in euros

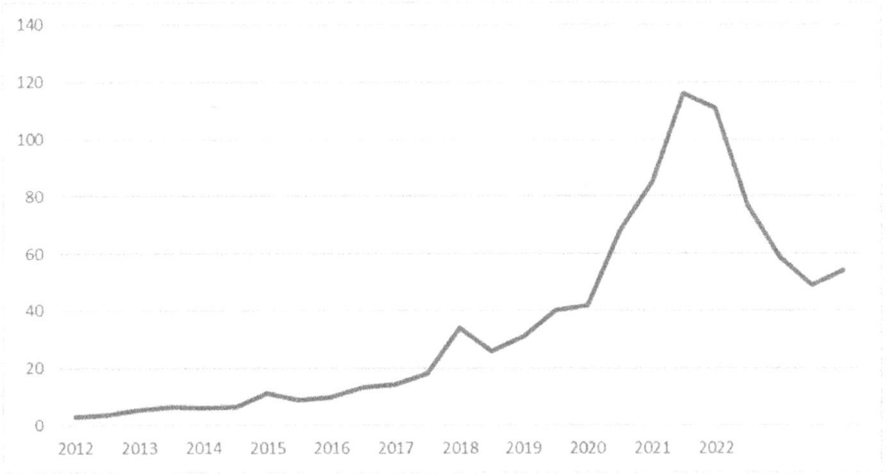

69. TRINET GROUP

WKN: 580884 ISIN: US16411R2085

One Park Place Suite 600, Dublin, CA 94568, **USA**

INTERNET HTTPS://WWW.TRINET.COM

Company

TRINET GROUP is a professional employer organization, that provides small and medium-size businesses with payroll and health benefits services and advises clients on employment law compliance and risk reduction. TRINET GROUP offers access to human capital expertise, benefits, risk mitigation and compliance, payroll and real-time technology.

Over the past six years, TRINET has gained an average of **28% p.a.**, and **42%** over the **last 12 months.**

TRINET GROUP share chart (2016 - 2022) in US-dollar

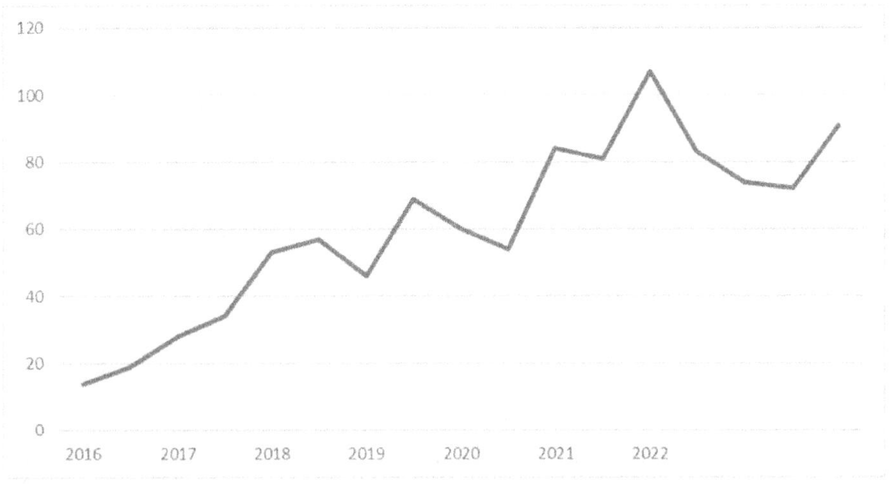

70.   TYLER TECHNOLOGIES INC

WKN: 917099 ISIN: US9022521051

5101 TENNYSON PARKWAY PLANO, TEXAS 75024

INTERNET   HTTPS://WWW.TYLERTECH.COM/

Company

TYLER TECHNOLOGIES INC. is a provider of Information Technology, Internet Services, IT Consulting Hardware, IT Services, Software industry to the United States public sector. The range of products offered by TYLER TECHNOLOGIES INC. includes appraisal and tax software, integrated software for courts and justice agencies, data and insights services, enterprise financial software systems, planning/regulatory/maintenance software, public safety software, records/document management software, and transportation software for schools. Tyler Technologies has offices in 17 states and one in Toronto, Ontario, Canada.

Over the past ten years, TYLER TECHNOLOGIES has gained an average of **25% p.a.**, and 28% over the last 12 months.

TYLER TECHNOLOGIES INC share chart (2016 - 2022) in euros

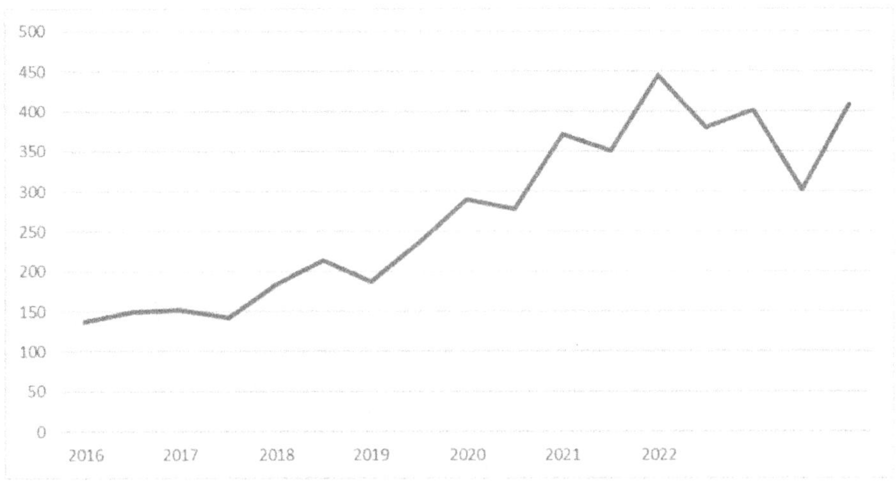

71. UFP TECHNOLOGIES

WKN: 902673102 ISIN: US9026731029

100 Hale Street Newburyport, MA 01950, **USA**

INTERNET   HTTPS://WWW.UFPT.COM/

Company

UFP TECHNOLOGIES is primarily a medical designer and manufacturer of custom devices, sub-assemblies, components and packaging utilizing highly specialized foams, films, and plastics. Their single-use and single-patient devices and components are used in a wide range of medical devices, disposable wound care, infection prevention, minimally invasive surgery, wearables, orthopedic soft goods, and orthopedic implant packaging. The company also supplies engineered products and components to customers in the automotive, aerospace, defense, consumer, electronics and industrial markets. Applications for its products include components for military uniforms and equipment, automotive interior trim, sports padding, environmentally friendly protective packaging, air filters, nail files, and protective covers and inserts.

Over the past six years, UFP TECHNOLOGIES has gained an average of **19% p.a.**, and 81% over the last 12 months.

UFP TECHNOLOGIES share chart (2012 - 2022) in US-dollar

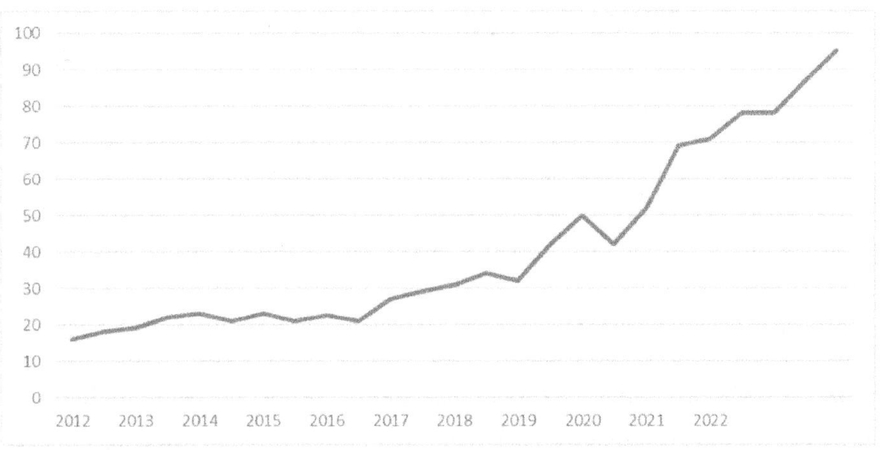

72.   UNION PACIFIC CORP.

WKN: 858144 ISIN: US907818108

DOUGLAS STREET 1400 68179 OMAHA, NEBRASKA, **USA**

INTERNET   HTTP://WWW.UP.COM

Company

UNION PACIFIC CORP. is one of the leading transportation companies in the USA, primarily active in the areas of freight transportation by rail. Union Pacific Railroad is the Group's most important operating company. The railroad company, with routes in 23 U.S. states, links the western coalfields, the agricultural growing region and the chemical industry of the Gulf Coast to the rail network and transports energy sources, raw materials, chemicals, metals and minerals, as well as foodstuffs, automobiles and consumer goods. In addition, the Group holds shares in associated technology companies and insurance companies.

Over the past ten years, UNION PACIFIC has gained an average of **16% p.a.**, and 31% over the last 12 months.

UNION PACIFIC CORP. share chart (2012 - 2022) in euros

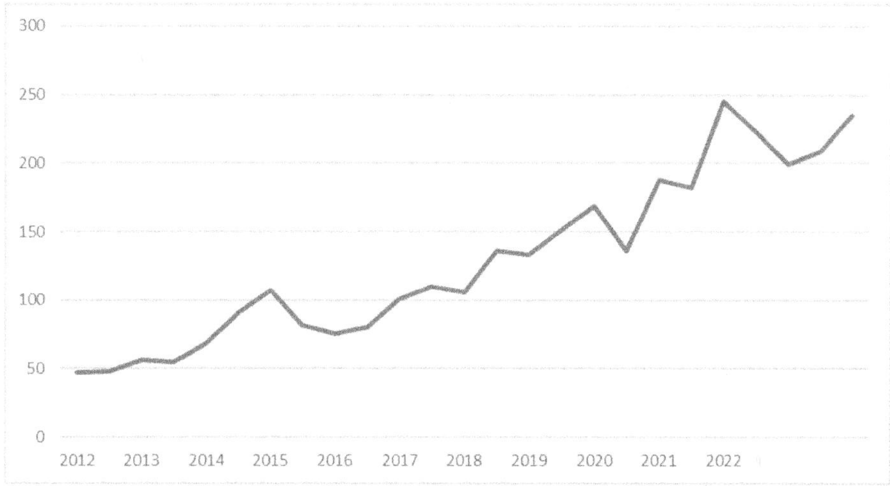

73.   VERISK ANALYTICS INC.

WKN: A0YA2M ISIN: US92345Y1064

WASHINGTON BOULEVARD 545 07310-1686 JERSEY CITY, NJ, **USA**

INTERNET   HTTP://WWW.VERISK.COM

Company

VERISK ANALYTICS INC. is a global risk analyst that provides risk assessments and decision models for many different industries including insurance, financial services, healthcare, government, and human resources. VERISK ANALYTICS INC.'s product offerings are specifically targeted to clients in the property insurance sector, as well as insurers and reinsurers. Organizations, government institutions and the risk management departments of companies in all industries are also customers of the company. In addition, VERISK ANALYTICS INC. offers solutions for the creation of decision models that enable the prediction of future potential losses as well as the recording of losses that have already occurred.

Over the past ten years, VERISK ANALYTICS has gained an average of **16% p.a.**, and 35% over the last 12 months.

VERISK ANALYTICS INC share chart (2012 - 2022) in euros

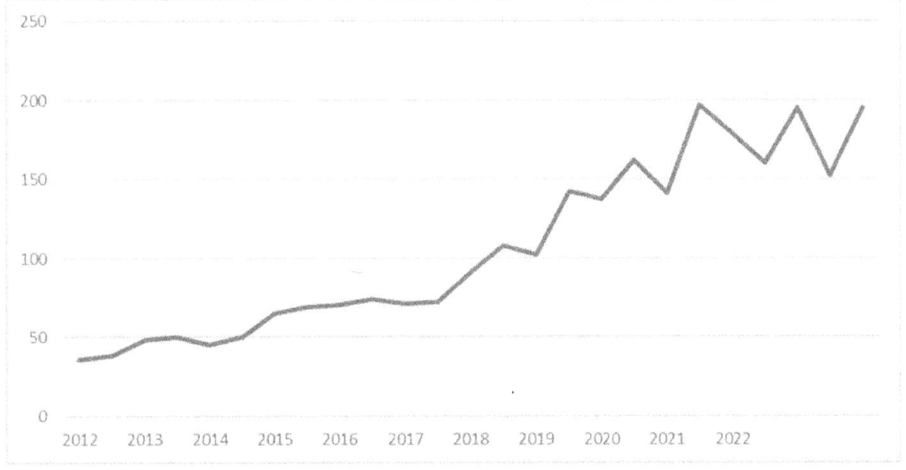

74.   VISA INC.

WKN: A0NC7B ISIN: US92826C8394

P.O. BOX 8999 94128, SAN FRANCISCO, CALIFORNIA, **USA**

INTERNET   HTTPS://USA.VISA.COM/

Company

VISA INC. is an internationally active credit card organization that offers electronic payment systems to banks in more than 20 countries. These include credit cards under the Visa, PLUS and Interlink brands. The Visa cards can be used worldwide and are currency-independent. In addition, the company is also active in the development of new technologies with regard to e-commerce and mobile payment, in order to work out secure and individual payment methods.

Over the past ten years, VISA has gained an average of **21% p.a.**, and 27% over the last 12 months.

VISA INC. share chart (2014 - 2022) in euros

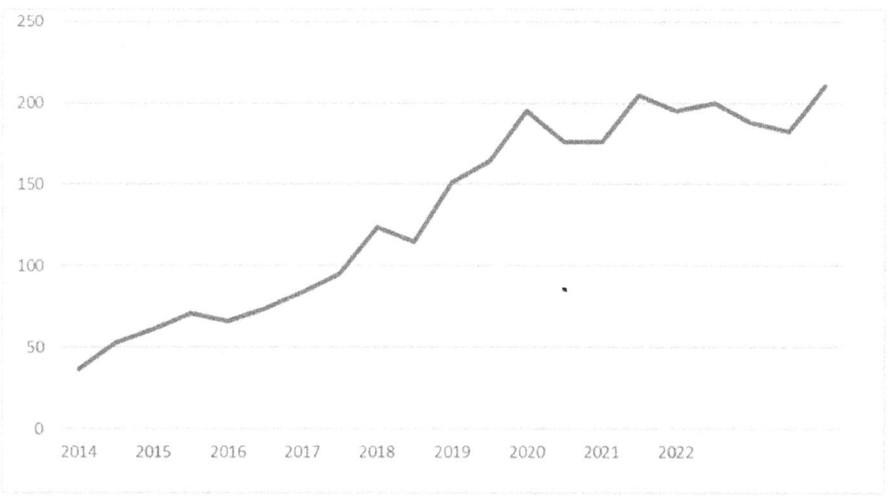

75.   WALMART INC.

WKN: 860853 **ISIN:** US9311421039

702 SW 8th St. Bentonville, Arkansas 72716, **USA**

INTERNET   https://stock.walmart.com

Company

WALMART INC. is a multinational retail group. The company operates in three segments: Walmart U.S., Walmart International, and Sam's Club. It operates supercenters, supermarkets, hypermarkets, warehouse clubs, cash-and-carry stores, and discount stores, warehouse clubs. The group sells products such as groceries, clothing, housewares, books, electronic devices, auto accessories, furniture, pet food, accessories, toys, cosmetics and jewelry through a global network of its own supermarkets and department stores. The company operates approximately 10,500 stores and various e-commerce websites under 46 brands in the North American region, as well as in Argentina, Brazil, Canada, China, Germany, Korea, Mexico, Puerto Rico and the United Kingdom.

Over the past ten years, WALMART has gained an average of **10% p.a.**, and 22% over the last 12 months.

WALMART INC. share chart (2013 - 2023) in euros

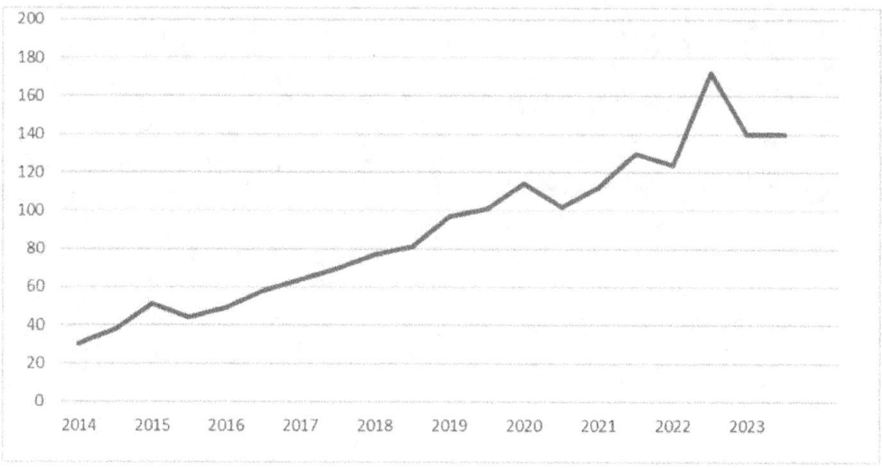

WASTE MANAGEMENT INC.

WKN: 893579 **ISIN:** US94106L1098

800 Capitol Street, Suite 3000 Houston, Texas 77002, **USA**

INTERNET   https://wm.com

Company

WASTE MANAGEMENT INC. is a provider of comprehensive waste management services such as waste collection services, waste transportation and disposal, recycling or conversion of waste into energy. Recipients of these services include private households, businesses, governmental entities, other waste collection companies, and electric utilities. The company maintains its own landfills, temporary storage facilities and recycling plants.

Over the past nine years, WASTE MANAGEMENT has gained an average of **17% p.a.**, and 35% over the last 12 months.

WASTE MANAGEMENT INC. share chart (2013 - 2023) in euros

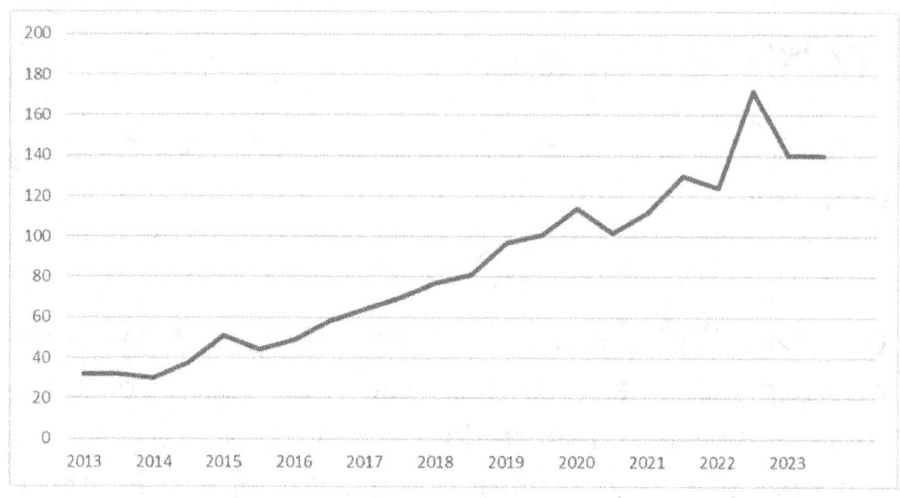

77.   WINMARK CORP.

WKN: 974250102 **ISIN:** US9742501029

605 Highway 169 N, Minneapolis, MN 55441, **USA**

INTERNET   https://winmarkcorporation.com/

Company

WINMARK CORP. is a franchisor specializing in the buying and selling of used merchandise. The company buys and sells used clothing and accessories for teens and young adults, children's clothing, toys, furniture, equipment and accessories, sporting goods, equipment and accessories for various sports activities, women's clothing, musical instruments, speakers, amplifiers, music-related electronics and related accessories. WINMARK CORP. serves small businesses in the United States and Canada.

Over the past six years, WINMARK has gained an average of **19% p.a.,** and 35% over the last 12 months.

WINMARK CORP. share chart (2013 - 2023) in US-dollar

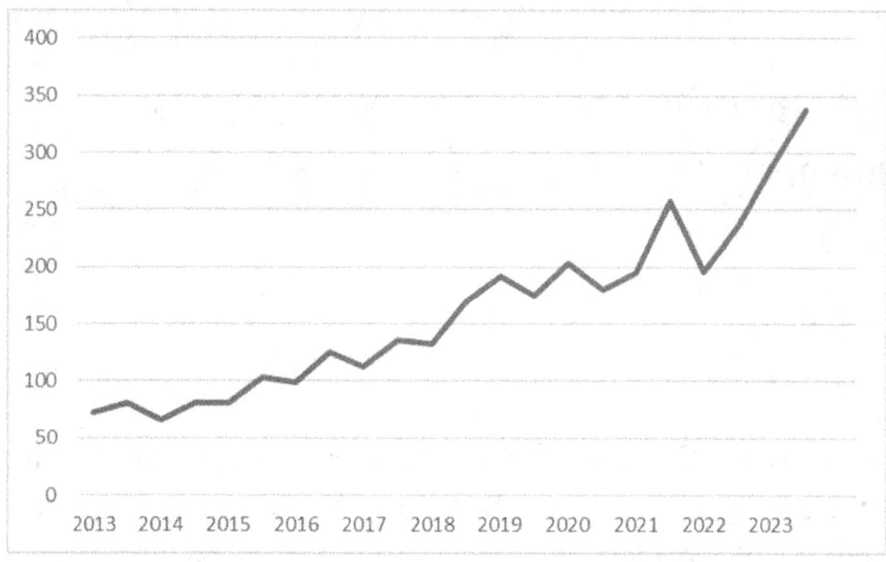

78.   WISETECH GLOBAL LTD

WKN: A2AGET **ISIN:** AU000000WTC3

74 O'Riordan Street, Alexandria NSW 2015, **AUSTRALIA**

INTERNET   https://www.wisetechglobal.com

Company

WISETECH GLOBAL LTD is a leading developer and provider of software solutions that help customers optimize their supply chain across all modes and borders.

Over the past seven years, WISETECH GLOBAL has gained an average of **48% p.a.**, and 33% over the last 12 months.

WISETECH GLOBAL LTD share chart (2016 - 2023) in euros

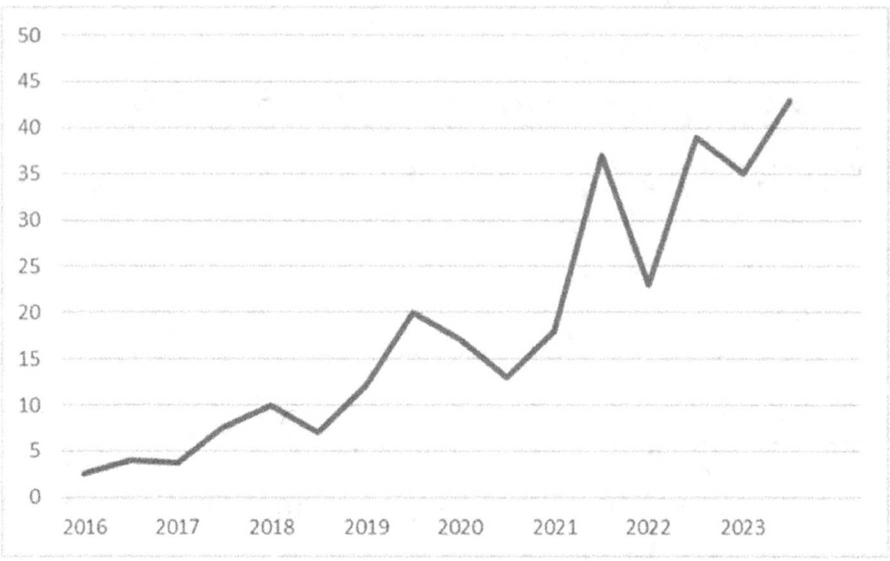

79.   WOLTERS KLUWER NV

WKN: A0J2R1 **ISIN:** NL0000395903

Zuidpoolsingel 2 2408 ZE Alphen aan den Rijn, **The Netherlands**

INTERNET   https://www.wolterskluwer.com

Company

WOLTERS KLUWER NV is a provider of expert information, software solutions and services for clinicians, auditors, lawyers, and tax, finance, audit, risk, compliance and regulatory professionals. The company's range of services is offered in the Netherlands, the rest of Europe, the United States, Canada, Asia Pacific and internationally.

Over the past six years, WOLTERS KLUWER has gained an average of **21% p.a.**, and 36% over the last 12 months.

WOLTERS KLUWER NV share chart (2013 - 2023) in euros

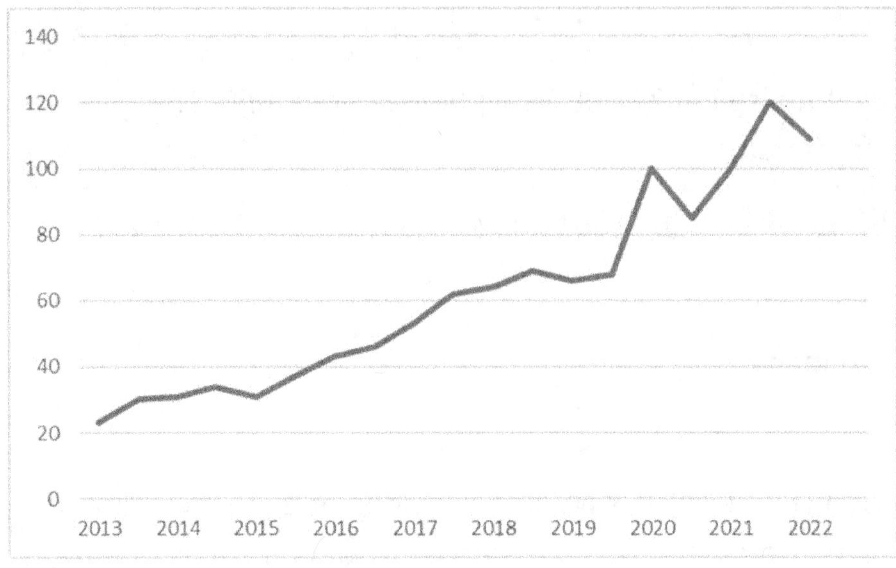

80.   WSP GLOBAL INC.

WKN: A1XBPS **ISIN:** CA92938W2022

1600 Boulevard René-Lévesque West, Montréal, Québec,
CANADA

INTERNET   https://www.wsp.com

Company

WSP GLOBAL INC is an international consulting firm with operations in the United States, Canada, United Kingdom, Sweden, Australia. WSP GLOBAL INC plans, designs and manages sustainable engineering solutions in the fields of earth and environment, energy and resources, industry, real estate and buildings, transport and infrastructure, and hydraulic engineering projects. The company's clients are public and private clients as well as construction companies.

Over the past nine years, WSP GLOBAL has gained an average of **21% p.a.**, and 20% over the last 12 months.

WSP GLOBAL INC. share chart (2014 - 2023) in euros

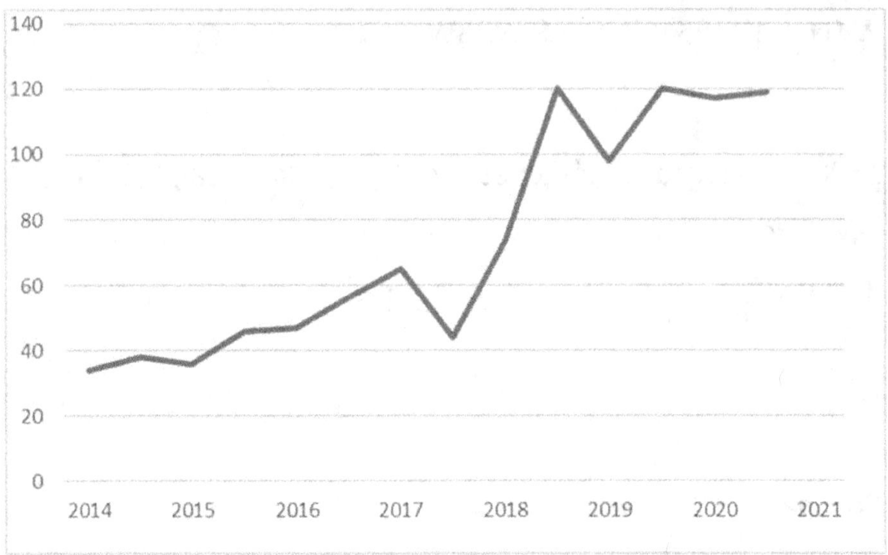

COMPANY	ISIN	Homepage	AIY*	SPI12 **
ADVANTEST CORP.	IE00B4BNMY34	http://www.accenture.com	+23%	+34%
ARISTA NETWOKS	US0404131064	https://www.arista.com/	+35%	+111 %
ARM HLDGS	US0420682058	https://www.arm.com/	-	+123 %
BOOKING HLD.	US09857L1089	https://www.bookingholdings.com/	+10%	+36%
COPART INC.	US2172041061	https://www.copart.com/	+29%	+51%
CROWDSTRIKE HLD.	US22788C1053	https://www.crowdstrike.com	-	+155 %
FAIR ISAAC CORP.	US3032501047	https://www.fico.com/	+38%	+89%
FERRARI N.V.	NL0011585146	https://www.ferrari.com/	+31%	+61%
FORTINET INC.	US34959E1091	https://www.fortinet.com	+32%	+19%
JABIL	US34959E1091	https://www.jabil.com/	+24%	+75%
MARSH+MCLENNAN COS.INC.	US5717481023	https://www.marshmclennan.com/	+16%	+25%
META PLATF.	US30303M1027	https://www.meta.com/	+23%	+188 %
MOTOROLA SOLUTIONS	US6200763075	https://www.motorolasolutions.com	+18%	+28%
NOVO-NORDISK AS	DK0062498333	https://www.novonordisk.de/	+22%	+69%
PULTE GROUP INC.	US7458671010	https://www.pultegroupinc.com	+20%	+105 %
ROYAL CARIBLR0008862868.CRUISES	LR0008862868	https://www.royalcaribbean.com	+9%	+73%
SAIA INC.	US78709Y1055	https://www.saia.com/	+33%	+103 %
SIMPSON MANUFACT.CO.	US8290731053	https://ir.simpsonmfg.com	+21%	+91%
SUPER MICRO COMPUT.	US86800U1043	https://www.supermicro.com	-	+820 %
TAIWAN SEMICON.MANU.	TW0002330008	https://www.taiwansemi.com	+27%	+50%

* Average share price increase per year over the last 10 years

** Share price increase over the last 12 months